S H A M E
Should Have Already Mastered Everything

How Unresolved Shame Gets in the Way of Our Humanity
(And What To Do About It)

Jane R. Pennington, M.A.

Illustrations by Charlie Lucker

Copyright © 2015 Jane R. Pennington M.A.
All rights reserved.

ISBN: 0692522859
ISBN 13: 9780692522851

Preface

In this workbook, SHAME: *Should Have Already Mastered Everything: How Unresolved Shame Gets in the Way of Our Humanity (and What to Do About It)*, the model I call Constellations of Possible Escape (COPE), is a blending of real life observations over years of study, the character defects described in 12 Step literature, and the works of five authors.

The concepts in the works of these five authors embrace a similar theme of shame dynamics that I also adhere to. Generally speaking, family therapist Virginia Satir uses the model of four "coping survival stances" used to protect against the pain of low self-esteem; psychiatrist Donald Nathanson uses four defensive strategies that comprise the compass of shame; psychoanalyst, Karen Horney employs "four major attempts of the neurotic individual to come to solution"; psychologist, Gershen Kaufman explains the foundation of shame through the lens of Silvan Tomkin's governing scenes and scripts, in addition to the idea of interpersonal need shame-binds; and Tony Webb honored his men's group experiences as they described their reaction to shame as hiding from self and others. Thank you, Tony for lending me those terms. Tony Webb also brought both an historical and social context to the study of shame dynamics.

Although these authors' work is highly valuable in the understanding of shame dynamics, their writings are written at a high literacy level primarily meant for professionals in the fields of psychology or social work, and therefore, out of reach for the layman. Furthermore, the solutions presented are vague and limited. It is fine to tell someone to love themselves, but how do they actually *do* that? For me, the solution came from 12 Step and Buddhist literature that encourages conscious noticing without judgment and a daily practice of simple, wholesome principles. In Part II of the workbook, the Wise-Self practices are based on the principles found in the 12 Step literature of Alanon and Alcoholics Anonymous and eastern psychology. In formulating this workbook I want to acknowledge the influence from all of these authors' works and the literature of Alcoholics Anonymous and Alanon, including Kevin Griffin's take on the 12 Steps of AA through a Buddhist framework.

The basic themes expressed in this work are: Humans develop, over the course of their lives, defensive strategies to avoid feeling shame --- a sense of deficiency or inadequacy. These strategies are ways of coping with shame and can become a habit. However, if our lives are lived continuously from the stance of defensively coping, then our daily lives easily become fractured, painful, unfulfilling, and fraught with distress and unhappiness with ourselves in addition to continued difficulties with relationships.

One of the primary aims of this workbook is to simplify complex ideas written about shame dynamics and to include everyday practices that will aid in increasing awareness and change engrained habits. The theory is simple: become more aware, practice different ways of doing, thinking, and feeling, become more aware, continue to practice.

In Part II of the workbook, The Wise-Self practices and other exercises, are suggestions of how to do things differently so there is more connection, stability, and caring in one's life. The practices are a place to continually **return to**. They are not a set of goals. They are ways of behaving, thinking, and feeling that help keep us in touch with our humanity and provide the guidance to help live a wholesome life. In order to have a wholesome life, one must practice wholesome ways.

I am grateful for the real-life experience of participating in 12 Step work for 29 years culminating in realizations about my own shame processes. Furthermore, my exposure to meditation and eastern psychology since 1988 has broadened what it means for me to be a human being. In addition, I am also very grateful for the insights gained from working with incarcerated individuals for over seven years. As they went through their struggles in completing in-prison programs they helped me build the exercises in this workbook and also helped me realize that a workbook on shame is crucial to gaining a solid foothold in life.

Jane R. Pennington
Author

Table of Contents

Introduction xi

    Why a workbook on shame? xi

    The Definition of Shame: xi

    Some of the Why's and How's of Shame xi

    Shame Pathways in our Brains xii

    What is unresolved shame? xiii

    The Challenge: Waking Up xiii

    The Practice of Being Your Wise-Self xiv

    Two Basic Parts to the Workbook xv

    Summary xvi

Part One 1

    Constellations of Possible Escape (COPE) 3

        Why a Constellation? 3

        Definitions of each Constellation 4

        Example of Moving Around the Constellations 5

        Working with the Constellations 5

        Suggestions on how to use Part One 5

Beginning Self-Reflection Exercises for working
with the Constellations of Possible Escape: How we COPE 7

Constellation #1 Invalidate Others 9

Constellation #1 Invalidate Others 11

    A Real Life Story 12

Self-Reflection Exercises For Invalidate Others 13

    Self-Reflection: Exercise #1 15

    Self-Reflection Exercise #2 for Invalidate Others 18

    Self-Reflection Exercise #3 for Invalidate Others 20

    Self-Reflection Exercise #4 for Invalidate Others 22

    Awareness Exercises for Invalidate Others 23

Constellation #2 Invalidate Self 25

Constellation #2 Invalidate Self 27

    Real Life Stories 28

Self-Reflection Exercises For Invalidate Self 29

    Self-Reflection Exercise #1 for Invalidate Self 31

    Self-Reflective Exercise #2 Invalidate Self 33

    Self-Reflection Exercise #3 Invalidate Self 34

    Self-Reflection Exercise #4 Invalidate Self 35

    Awareness Exercises for Invalidate Self 36

Constellation #3 Hide from Self 37

Constellation #3 Hide from Self 39

    A Real Life Story 40

Self-Reflection Exercises for Hide from Self · · · 41

Self-Reflection Exercise #1 for Hide from Self · · · 43

Self-Reflection Exercise #2 Hide from Self · · · 46

Self-Reflection Exercise #3 Hide from Self · · · 47

Self-Reflection Exercise #4 Hide from Self · · · 48

Awareness Exercises for Hide from Self · · · 49

Constellation #4 Hide from Others · · · 51

Constellation #4 Hide from Others · · · 53

A Real Life Story · · · 54

Self-Reflection Exercises for Hide from Others · · · 55

Self-Reflection Exercise #1 for Hide from Others · · · 57

Self-Reflection Exercise #2 Hide from Others · · · 60

Self-Reflection Exercise #3 Hide from Others · · · 61

Self-Reflection Exercise #4 Hide from Others · · · 62

Self-Reflection Exercise #5 Hide from Others · · · 63

Awareness Exercises for Hide from Others · · · 64

Part Two · · · 65

Being Your Wise-Self is a Process · · · 67

Being Your Wise-Self · · · 69

Four Ways of Being Your Wise-Self · · · 69

Examples of Practicing Being Your Wise-Self · · · 70

Working with being your Wise-Self · · · 72

Suggestions on how to use Part Two 73

Beginning Self-Reflection Exercises for Being Your Wise-Self 75

    Beginning Self-Reflection Exercise #1 77

    Beginning Self-Reflection Exercise #2 78

    Beginning Self-Reflection Exercise #3 79

Respect Others 81

Respect Others 83

    Real Life Stories 84

    Self-Reflection Exercise #1 for Respect Others 86

    Self-Reflection Exercise #2 for Respect Others 86

    Self-Reflection Exercise #3 for Respect Others 87

    Self-Reflection Exercise #4 for Respect Others 88

    Awareness Exercises for Respect Others 89

    Practices for Respect Others 90

Respect Self 91

Respect Self 93

    Real Life Stories 94

    Self-Reflection Exercise #1 for Respect Self 96

    Self-Reflection Exercise #2 Respect Self 96

    Self-Reflection Exercise #3 Respect Self 97

    Self-Reflection Exercise #4 for Respect Self 98

    Self Reflection Exercise #5 for Respect Self 99

- Awareness Exercises for Respect Self · 100
- Practices for Respect Self · 101

Present with Self · 103

Present with Self · 105

- Real Life Stories · 106
- Self-Reflection Exercise #1 for Present with Self · 108
- Self-Reflection Exercise #2 Present with Self · 109
- Self-Reflection Exercise #3 Present with Self · 110
- Self-Reflection Exercise #4 Present with Self · 111
- Awareness Exercises for Present with Self · 112
- Practices for Present with Self · 113

Present with Others · 115

Present with Others · 117

- A Real Life Story · 118
- Self-Reflection Exercise #1 for Present with Others · 119
- Self-Reflection Exercise #2 Present with Others · 120
- Self-Reflection Exercise #3 Present with Others · 121
- Self-Reflection Exercise #4 Present with Others · 122
- Awareness Exercises for Present with Others · 123
- Practices for Present with Others · 124

Appendices · 125

- The Vocabulary of Shame · 127

The Ranges of Shame · 128

Shame Log · 129

Alphabetical List of Shame Labels · 130

Feeling Faces · 131

Shame-Busting Statements · 132

Introduction

Why a workbook on shame?

The reason that mending our shame wounds is the most important work a human being can do is because it brings us face to face with our humanity. Learning how to value our humanity, and accept our humanness, restores us to sanity.

When we avoid our unresolved shame we navigate through our personal relationships and social interactions on automatic pilot using ingrained, habitual reactions that disconnect us from ourselves and others.

Continuously defending against a sense of inferiority, we deny ourselves the opportunity to really know who we are and care for ourselves. We miss out on the comfort and reward of fulfilling relationships, satisfying work, and orderly and sane lives. Instead our lives have constant go-rounds of bitterness, anger, rage, shame, isolation, discouragement, despair, contempt for our self and others, self-hate and substance abuse. Our habitual strategies protect us and feed the drama, chaos and unease in our life.

It is the objective of this workbook to help you increase your awareness of the habitual strategies used to avoid shame. The exercises will offer you ways to start noticing your reactions as they occur. Once you start observing and noticing, you can then begin to practice wholesome behaviors that lead you to your Wise Self. A Wise-Self is an aware self. A Wise-Self is assertive and not aggressive, is kind and giving and understanding to others while maintaining good boundaries, works to stay connected with self and others by reaching out and not hiding away, refrains from harmful behavior, thoughts and feelings and practices shame-busting self-talk that uplifts and keeps their thinking positive.

The Definition of Shame:

Shame is defined as: the feeling or sense of being deficient and unworthy as a human being; the belief that the essence of who we are is somehow defective. In addition to this deep sense of inadequacy, we fear that these defects, this brokenness, will now be revealed and then judged by others who will then confirm our unworthiness.

Some of the Why's and How's of Shame

A person with a continuous reoccurring sense of inadequacy and unworthiness has a shame-centered identity. This shame centered-identity usually results from continually receiving the message that you have little or no value as a person and/or your natural human needs and drives are demeaned and disallowed by others. You are *not* cherished for being "just you." This de-valuing can occur from ages 0 to 3 or enter into our lives at grade school age, as teenagers, young adults, mid-life, and old age.

Most likely the pattern of de-valuing started very young. Care givers provide the primary interactions that contribute to creating a shame-centered identity. (For more on this read Pia Mellody, "Facing Codependence.") If our care givers (parents, teachers, ministers, scout leaders, coaches, and others of significance to us) are in denial about their own shame, then in the course of an interaction with the child, they avoid the pain of their shame, by handing their shame to the child. *The shame in these care givers is unresolved because it has never been acknowledged as theirs.* Quite often handing their unresolved shame over to the children in their care is done without any awareness on their part. These caregivers are numb to their shame.

In this way having a shame-centered identity is generational, passing from one adult set of caregivers with unresolved shame to their children; those children grow up and pass their shame on to their children.

Here is an example of how unresolved shame gets passed from a father to a son:

A father shows contempt to his son (through what he says, the tone of his voice, the look on his face, his body postures, his actions) whenever his son expresses a need. This son grows up with self-hate and loathing. Anytime he has a need, for example, like the need to feel recognized and appreciated or the need to be touched, he will feel deeply undeserving of this legitimate and very human trait. He then acts toward himself in a similar way he experienced his father, such as ignoring the need, pretending he doesn't really have the need, or berating himself when the need does arise. A shame-centered identity can now develop around the expressing of his needs. When this son has a son who expresses needs, as a father he will disallow and shame his son for those needs.

Kaufman, Gershen, (1996). <u>The Psychology of Shame: Theory and Treatment of Shame-Based Syndromes</u>. New York: Springer Publishing Company, Inc.

Shame Pathways in our Brains

Often we find ourselves in situations where our reactions are very strong or intense, and/or they are frequent (we have the same reaction very often) and/or the reaction lasts for a long time like having something "eat at you" for days, unable to let it go.

The reason for all of this is because each time shame is triggered the pathways in our brains try to find similar patterns of experience from our past. Our neurological structure stores similar, past shame experiences in groups or clumps. So when some shame experience in the present resembles some shame experience from the past we react based on the pathways set down by our neurological histories (just like when a car travels over the same dirt road again, again, the road becomes worn by the path of the car). This means that if shame continually goes unresolved, it becomes what is called toxic, or chronic, and we develop a shame-centered identity.

Nathanson, Donald L. (1992). <u>Shame and Pride: Affect, Sex, and the Birth of the Self.</u> New York: W.W. Norton and Company

Kaufman, Gershen, (1996). <u>The Psychology of Shame: Theory and Treatment of Shame-Based Syndromes</u>. New York: Springer Publishing Company, Inc.

The storing of shame experiences can be done in three separate ways or in all three ways together. 1) Through images, 2) through language, and 3) through emotions. You see a look on someone's face and it registers as that look your mother gave you and shame is triggered. Or, you hear a tone of voice and your neurological pathways send you the message that the voice sounds a lot like when Dad talked down to you and it triggers shame, or your teacher uses a certain word and you notice that you don't feel so confident anymore, or, you get mad at your sweetheart so she backs off, but you aren't really mad, you just want to keep her at a distance. You believe that if she sees you as you really are she won't love you. Inside your self-talk says: "She could never love me." Alas, a sense of inadequacy has reared its head blocking the connection and flow of love to someone you care about.

What is unresolved shame?

Shame is unresolved when we use certain strategies to deny, avoid, hide, or cover up our *sense* of deficiency and unworthiness. We choose to camouflage our shame feelings through strategies that include bullying others physically and verbally, seeking power and control over others, constantly judging others or lashing out against ourselves by continually putting ourselves down, and finding ways to prove we are unworthy. Other strategies include being purposely unavailable to others and not participating fully in life; or in yet another strategy we try to dissolve our unresolved shame with drugs or alcohol, over-work, over spending and over eating. All of these strategies numb our humanness. However, our shame moves into resolution each time we notice and acknowledge our shame and how it plays out in our lives. It is our responsibility to learn about our own shame patterns. Only then can we begin to practice more wholesome ways of living and relating.

Unresolved shame indicates that life is being lived unconsciously, unaware, and on autopilot. There is an unwillingness to look or discover the reality of what is occurring *in us*. In our unresolved shame we often have very little tolerance for emotional distress, yet we create bigger messes in our lives by employing defensive strategies to "manage" the distress. We may also feel that others can see what we *believe* to be our unworthiness and deficiency and that once they see this we will be rejected and denied approval, acceptance, and love. The fear of having our believed unworthiness exposed increases the use of our defenses, and keeps our shame unresolved.

The Challenge: Waking Up

"Awareness is the greatest agent of change."
Eckhart Tolle *A New Earth: Awakening to Your Life's Purpose*

To make matters more challenging, we are often very unaware of the defensive and self-protective strategies we use to avoid unresolved shame. This is because ingrained, deep-seated habits have become automatic. They are so automatic that we often believe that this is "just the way I am." Even though the way we react to life's circumstances does not work for us, we continue to let our defensive strategies go unexamined. Not knowing how to make a change, we often believe our reactions are fixed in stone, and we are stuck. We lead lives that are full of anger, sarcasm, and grumpiness. We keep an emotional distance from others, we close ourselves off from our feelings, don't share or connect, and stay shut down and isolated.

When our unresolved shame is in play we become estranged from others, sometimes getting caught up in an unending cycle of disrespect and anger. Often we blame others as the sole cause of our hurt and we focus completely outward, pointing to the part that others played in the interaction. We are relieved, believing that blaming absolves us from any examination or awareness of ourselves. The pain is temporarily gone. We are "off the hook" because we have laid it on the other guy.

With unresolved shame driving our motives and actions we distance ourselves from our own innate goodness and in addition never see the humanness in others. Our life becomes full of striving to continually dominate and control others or we employ tactics that keep us walled-off and isolated from others. We abuse substances, hide from ourselves and others with busyness and any means to "save face" by looking good on the outside, while on the inside we are barely glued together.

Want to start to wake up? Turn to the Appendices and do the Vocabulary of Shame Exercise and the Ranges of Shame Exercise. Share your self-discovery with someone you feel emotionally safe with and will listen to you without judgment.

The Practice of Being Your Wise-Self

Bill P., Todd W., and Sara S. from the book *Drop the Rock* say that "your true right-size is the middle ground between grandiosity and intense shame." In other words, a middle ground is a place that embraces humility. In humility we have learned to gently own our part in the scheme of things, maintain our integrity, stay vital and awake, have regard for others, and participate wholesomely in life.

Similarly, Pia Mellody, who is an addiction counselor, refers to "the size you really are" in her book *The Ground Rules for Overcoming the Obstacles to Truth, Respect, and Lasting Love*:

> When we experience our own shame, we believe that someone has seen us as we really are – human and imperfect. When you can feel your own shame, you know that you are not a god or goddess…it helps you speak with humility. It keeps you the size you really are.

As you will see, being our Wise-Self is all about being "the size you really are." When we **COPE** and are caught up in a Constellation of Possible Escape from our unresolved shame, we either puff ourselves up to be more than others, or we deflate ourselves to be less than others. Neither strategy embraces any humility and we distance ourselves from our own and other's humanness.

> ***This workbook suggests that we develop a practice of stepping back; giving space to whatever feels defective, abiding the discomfort, distress and unpleasantness and noticing our sense of deficiency, all the while with a non-judgmental and gentle awareness. Everything that comes up for us can then be our teacher.***

The choice to embrace our humanity opens the way for us to live a more wholesome life. Choosing to engage in the process of repairing our shame wounds can be the restoration of our sanity, leaving painful loneliness and alienation behind. As we learn to practice being our Wise-Self we start to re-program our responses to our life situations and the people around us. This often leads to more connection with others and increased compassion for ourselves.

Gaining sanity has one hitch: we have to begin to do some work. It is just like making the effort to exercise your body every day. Doing the pull-ups, sit-ups, and push-ups creates a gradual change in your physique, building well-defined muscle groups. Similarly, doing the exercises for shame work provided in this workbook will develop your "social-emotional" muscle. Our emotional life starts to become more solid and well-defined and this gives us the strength and flexibility we need to start to live our life differently as our Wise-Self.

Working with shame requires us to pay attention to uncomfortable emotions, defensive behaviors, and critical and judgmental thoughts. Shame work requires us to "wake-up" to what is going on within us. A day-to-day practice of awareness alongside wholesome actions to re-establish connection with ourselves and others is the work that will bring forth changes in behavior, thinking, and emotional management. This workbook provides specific ways to start practicing and developing our Wise-Self. It is an adventure that is worth every effort we put into it.

The work is challenging and demands the willingness to notice our feelings, body sensations and gestures, behaviors, and thinking patterns. The *practice of noticing* takes time to develop. The secret to creating sanity in our lives – but the one thing many of us do not want to do – is to daily *practice noticing* what arises around our shame. This work also calls for us to be brave. Mending our shame starts with the courage to see ourselves as we really are, and no matter what we notice, to abide with what comes up for us, observing it with interest and a willingness to listen "wholeheartedly" to what it may tell us. Wholeheartedness is described by psychiatrist Karen Horney as, "to be without pretense, to be emotionally sincere, to be able to put the whole of oneself into one's feelings, one's work, one's beliefs." (p. 242, *Our Inner Conflicts*)

The work we do with unresolved shame can take us to deep and strange places. If we are bold enough to go to those places, personal transformation can begin. We will discover that some of the keys to transformation are awareness, noticing, observing, identifying or naming, and a practice of building emotional tolerance.

Two Basic Parts to the Workbook

Part One
Awareness of Constellations of Possible Escape (COPE)

Constellations of Possible Escape are the strategies and tactics we use to avoid and defend against our unresolved shame. These Constellations are patterns of behavior, thinking, and emotion that we use to *escape* the pain of unresolved shame. These patterns keep us from our Wise (and true) Self. They are the road blocks to wholesome living.

The first step in our work is to recognize and increase awareness of your strategies and tactics to avoid unresolved shame. The Awareness Exercises encourage you to practice awareness three ways: through body, thought, and feeling. The Self-Reflection Exercises recommend writing or list making and drawing or collage to recognize your defense habits more clearly. The Self-Reflection Exercises may also be used for discussion in a group or individual counseling.

In Part One of the book you will learn how to:

Acknowledge your unresolved shame through *gentle awareness* of the four main strategies we use to defend against what we *believe to be* our inadequacies -- our "sore" spots.

Here is a list of the four Constellations Of Possible Escape (COPE)
See the definitions on p. 4. Each constellation has its own chapter with specific exercises.

1. **We invalidate others**
2. **We invalidate ourselves**
3. **We hide from ourselves**
4. **We hide from others**

Part Two
Practicing Being Your Wise-Self

As we move forward we are presented with four ways to practice being our Wise-Self. Through a different set of Self-Reflection and Awareness Exercises we get a chance to do things differently, think differently, and relate to our emotions differently. Again, awareness exercises encourage the focus on body, thought, and feeling in order to recognize change in habits. We continue to use our newly developed awareness skills enabling us to practice being our Wise-Self and live a more wholesome and skillful life. Self-Reflection exercises in Part Two include making lists, drawing, creating a collage, and meditation practices.

In Part Two we will move forward:

As shame is resolved through gentle awareness and acknowledgment we become more capable of *practicing being our Wise-Self.*

Here are the four primary ways to practice being our Wise-Self.
See the definitions on p. 70. Each Wise-Self way has its own chapter with exercises.

1. **We respect others**
2. **We respect ourselves**
3. **We stay present to ourselves**
4. **We stay present with others**

Summary

The key to dealing with unresolved shame is to increase our awareness of the habitual strategies we use to avoid shame. Often these habitual measures are unknown to us and hidden from the usual way we see ourselves and others.

These self-protective strategies feed our anger, sadness, unease, anxiety and increase the chaos in our lives. Their purpose is to keep us from the pain of seeing our deficiencies and to guard against others seeing them. The belief that the essence of who we are is somehow defective is called shame. It can become the center of our identity. Shame is unresolved when we consistently use strategies to COPE. COPE stands for Constellations of Possible Escape. These strategies are ways we turn away from acknowledging our unresolved shame and acceptance of who we really are. The result is conflicts, disputes, friction, and disharmony with ourselves and our relationships.

After we have practiced noticing and becoming aware of our habitual self-protective strategies we can begin to move forward into practicing being our Wise-Self. Being our Wise-Self is a process. It means that we have started to wake-up and are no longer using ingrained habitual responses. We start to introduce daily, wholesome actions into our lives replacing old habitual strategies of handling conflicts, ways we talk to others and ourselves, and certain negative ways of thinking. We are no longer grandiose or intensely full of shame and our center of identity is no longer purely defined by our unresolved shame.

We learn to embrace our humanity through awareness, noticing, observing, and practicing tolerance with our difficult emotions. As we practice being our Wise-Self, we are no longer estranged from ourselves or others. We own our stuff, stay honest, and become more loving and understanding thereby creating a more manageable and sane way to live.

Part One

Acknowledge your unresolved shame through *gentle awareness* of the strategies we use to defend against what we *believe to be* inadequate, defective, or insufficient.

Constellations of Possible Escape (COPE)

Why a Constellation?
Merriam-Webster.com defines a constellation as:
   A set of ideas, conditions, symptoms or traits that fall into or appear to fall into a pattern. An assemblage, collection or group of usually related qualities.

- Using a constellation as a model helps to see unresolved shame as a complex occurrence.
- We can use any strategy or combination of strategies explained below to escape from unresolved shame.
- Constellations of unresolved shame are grouping or patterns of behaviors, thinking, and emotions.
- We can use any one particular Constellation or any combination of two or three, or go from one to the other during the course of an experience.

As we will see in the more detailed explanations constellations represent ways of relating to ourselves and to the world around us. These ways are usually not effective and bring discord, anger, unhappiness, and disruption into our lives and relationships.   It is your job to become aware of when these constellations are in play in your life then change can begin.

Definitions of each Constellation

Invalidate Others Constellation #1
Our goal is to have control over others and display power over others. We must be seen as right and superior. Arguments are started to prove we are right and to admit an error is seen as weakness. We believe the saying: Might makes right. Insensitivity and hard-heartedness is strength.

Invalidate Self Constellation #2
Our goal is to be seen as less than in relation to others. We believe we deserve contempt *from* others. We find ways to give our power away. We constantly disregard our own worth. We see ourself as a victim.

Hide from Self Constellation #3
Our objective is to protect from our awareness any possible defect we believe we have. We deceive and manipulate others and ourself. We distract ourself from facing any defects of ourself that may surface. We are often dishonest with others and ourself. We will do almost anything to stay in denial and often become addicted to drugs, alcohol, food, gambling, shopping, or work.

Hide from Others Constellation #4
Our goal is to not have our inner self exposed for others to see because we are ashamed of our "self." The way this is managed is by isolating. We choose to have limited connection with others. We lead a "smaller" life because we hide ourself away for fear of what others may think.

Example of Moving Around the Constellations
Let's look at an example of one person moving from one Constellation to another in the course of one experience:

One evening Jim had an argument with his spouse, Sarah. It was a loud and nasty argument and he hurled insults at her blaming her very unjustly. Then Jim stormed out of the house and went to the local bar and drank a lot trying to avoid feelings that came up from the argument. He kept drinking to avoid feeling anything. He came back to the house and slept in the spare room, avoiding Sarah that evening and the next morning. When he woke up he told himself what a terrible person he is and that he will never be able to have a relationship.

How Jim moved from one Constellation to another:

- **Invalidate Others**: Blaming unjustly, starting a nasty argument
- **Hide from Self**: Using alcohol to numb and hide feelings from himself
- **Hide from Others**: Left the house to go to the bar and then slept in the spare room and avoided the spouse
- **Invalidate Self**: Used negative self-talk to judge and belittle himself.

Working with the Constellations
This is what we will find in the next few pages:

1) A two to three page description of each Constellation with a A Real Life Story for each
2) A set of Self-Reflection Exercises for each Constellation
3) One page of Awareness Exercises for each Constellation

Suggestions on how to use Part One

1) Take time to read about each Constellation
2) Start at least one of the Awareness Exercises for a week as soon as possible.
3) Check the list of behaviors in the first Self-Reflection Exercise for each Constellation for recognition and confirmation.
4) Do the Self-Reflection Exercises alongside the Awareness Exercises. These exercises require some writing or drawing and time in a quiet place to think honestly about the questions.

Beginning Self-Reflection Exercises for working with the Constellations of Possible Escape: How we COPE

Exercise #1
Look up the word *aware* in the dictionary or on-line and write down all of the definitions. Then, take a few minutes and **reflect how you are aware and how you *avoid* being aware**. Write down your reflections.

How I am aware:

How I avoid being aware:

Exercise #2
Read the summaries of the four Constellations on p. 4 and the Example of Moving Around the Constellations on p.16. Describe (or draw) a time in your life (current or past) that you moved from one Constellation to another similar to the example.

Exercise #3
Questions for discussion or to write or draw about:

1) How do you present yourself to others as "bigger than" or "more powerful than" (include family, friends co-workers)?
2) How do you express self-loathing and disdain? In what ways do you stay connected to those who undermine your self-worth?
3) How do you redirect attention away from yourself so people don't see your flaws? How do you avoid being honest with yourself? Is there any kind of substance over-use in your life?
4) How do you retreat and withdraw from participation (with family, friends or co-workers)? How does keeping distance from others keep you safe?

Constellation #1
Invalidate Others

Our goal is to have control and display power over others. We want to be seen as right and superior. Arguments are started to prove we are right and to admit and error is seen as weakness. We believe the saying: Might makes right. Insensitivity and hard heartedness is strength.

Constellation #1
Invalidate Others

To Invalidate Others is to present yourself as being bigger than and more powerful than others. This can be done in a variety of ways. First, there are physical attacks, such as hitting, punching, slapping, and spanking, etc. These actions are used to dominate and control someone else. Those who use Invalidate Others may bully or intimidate with words also. Name calling, swearing, putting someone down, and "hitting them below the belt" are common ways to invalidate and attack others. The major effort in this constellation is to maintain control over others. This sense of control and power helps us to avoid seeing the weakness and inferiority in ourselves. We have protected our insides with our aggressiveness for so long that we have now created a habit. We automatically move into verbal or physical bravado much like a peacock spreading its plume of feathers. We must make sure to preserve our image of power and control to ensure we are seen and believed to be "bigger than others."

One of the more understated ways to Invalidate Others is being a stuffy, stubborn, know-it-all. This is a way of maintaining an appearance of control and to continue to convince ourselves that we are worthy and powerful. A super-reasonable person is sometimes just really trying to manipulate others with information. In other words, the more I can show you what I know, the better I will look, and the worse you will look, because you don't know what I know!!

When we use data and information for power and control we push our intuitive and "feeling-self" aside. We come at others with facts, figures, and stories (or things others said that we have so carefully remembered and stored for use at just the right time). When we become a "know-it-all" we can be very quick, using our wit to control our interactions. We might not be swearing or nasty, maybe just a little jokingly sarcastic so we seem like we are being funny.

It is our intent that is questionable. Our intent is to keep others in their place; to keep them "one down." This way we can make them "the dumb gal or guy" and feel superior about ourselves. In the meantime others end up being very passive and quiet because Invalidate Others means we have bullied others into submission!!

Living life from the constellation of Invalidate Others provides great satisfaction for us because others have "submitted." It strokes our ego, keeps us safe, and gives us a personal sense of power. Others are not seen as humans who make mistakes and who can be forgiven. In Invalidate Others, people are seen as bad, not ok, less than. We use our attacks and techniques to prop ourselves up as better than, more ok than the other guy and to feel good about ourselves. We blame, laying all responsibility on others. We must win; we must be right. To do differently would be to reveal our vulnerable human self, perhaps too raw at times for us to experience. And, too emotionally dangerous for us to let others see.

In the constellation of Invalidate Others, we will do anything to show that we have power over someone else. Sometimes, just by habit, we put others down. We may say it jokingly and even say "Oh, I was only joking." But, we really weren't. In Invalidate Others we puff ourselves up and have no tolerance of being in a situation where we feel less than others or feel powerless. We position ourselves so that we are never "gotten the better of" which keeps us as the "big man" and the "top dog." Invalidate Others is the "I'll show them!" position. When we are in it or moving into it, we feel very powerful and our bodies are often full of adrenaline. We might not be aware of it, but we want to humiliate and shame. We want to scare or intimidate others (even just a bit) so they will keep their distance from us. We use Invalidate Others as a spear to attack while holding a shield to protect because we have convinced ourselves that we must safeguard some shameful spot inside of us that others must not see. We do not want anyone to get a hint of our humanness. Sadly, this often happens with those we actually want to connect with the most.

A Real Life Story
Sally tells this story about an interaction she had with a friend.

I remember having a conversation with someone and they were pointing out to me that I was not seeing another person in a positive light. They said that I was judging. When I heard this I felt judged and I heard a "should," as in you "should not judge others." I felt put in my place. In order to counter I came out with a "ya, but..." I didn't actually say "ya, but," however, what I did was to quickly point (with lots of bravado and one-ups-man-ship) out that I felt judged and that I believed they were doing to me what they were asking me *not* to do to others.

That didn't go over very well. Instead of staying open to hear what I was pointing out they shut down and would not communicate further. When I attempted to re-engage they got really, really mad and ended the interaction moving to another room.

Later when we purposely set aside sometime to discuss what happened the person told me that when I was making my point I had leaned toward them and they heard me as sharp and quick witted. They said they could not match my mental quickness at the time and felt less than and put down.

It took me awhile to own my part in this interaction. After all I was just pointing out what I saw as "the truth." But the way I did it really put the other person in their place. It didn't feel like I was doing that, but it was perceived as that. And when I examined the forces behind what I had said I could honestly say that my intent was not loving, kind, or helpful. This does not excuse the other person's anger, but it does show how our "personal radar" can easily pick up on the other person's subtle attempt to invalidate another.

Self-Reflection Exercises For Invalidate Others

In Invalidate Others your goal is to have control and display power over others. You want to be seen as being right and superior.

Self-Reflection: Exercise #1
Below is a list of 12 behaviors used to Invalidate Others.

a) Put a check next to ones that you have used. Add some of your own.
b) On the next page, write about 2 occasions when you use any of the behaviors listed. Reflect on the outcome.

1. When you listen you are gathering information and waiting for your opening to drive *your* point home.
2. You tease hard. You are belittling and intimidating. You choose strong language or name call or are vulgar.
3. You often "go for the jugular" or "hit below the belt" aiming at other's sensitive issues.
4. You are a know-it-all. You are the expert. You use logic and "data" to convince others. In a conversation you present yourself as "super-reasonable." You leave no room for other's opinions and you disallow the facts anyone else may bring up.
5. You find the flaw in what others are saying and expertly point this out. You feel better about yourself when you do this.
6. You slap, hit, punch, pick a fight, kick, push, or throw something (sometimes at someone).
7. With friends you often banter (mock and joke) with them. You will always make sure you are on the "winning" side and glorified by others who laugh with approval at your banter.
8. You retaliate when someone has touched a nerve. You may be truly threatening or vague. You feel powerful and do not want to be seen as weak.
9. You tell people how they feel. You make assumptions about their motives. You have them all figured out and cannot be second-guessed.
10. You gossip about others, putting others down. Gossip bonds you to those you gossip with. Gossip creates an "us" vrs "them." You are "us" and you are better than "them."
11. You think you have *the* answers to a problem. In an argument you are right; you hold on to your rightness tightly through being insistent. In an argument it is all about you. You must have the last word.
12. You interject or interrupt others in conversations. You counter what others say. Winning in a conversation is everything to you. Sometimes you start and argument or conflict just to be able to win your point.

13. _____

14. _____

Occasion#1

Occasion#2

Self-Reflection Exercise #2 for Invalidate Others

Describe 3 incidents when you have invalidated or attacked others. What words did you use? If you got physical in anyway, describe what you did. Name specific conduct you used to be powerful and in control.

a) _____

b) _____

c)

Self-Reflection Exercise #3 for Invalidate Others

Sometimes we feel shame because we see ourselves as abandoned or left out. This may bring up feelings of "not being good enough." Our partner or friends choose to spend time with others, choose to focus on their work, or choose to take time for them. This can bring up past events that were laid down in our childhood. More often than not, these past events were interpreted by us as indications that we were "not good enough" (otherwise people would spend time with us). That sense of "not good enough" is shame and we sometimes we choose to discharge the pain of not feeling good enough by lashing out.

Write about a time when you felt "not good enough" and avoided the painful feeling of shame with some kind of aggressive behavior.

_____
_____
_____
_____
_____
_____
_____
_____
_____
_____
_____
_____
_____
_____
_____
_____
_____

SHAME: SHOULD HAVE ALREADY MASTERED EVERYTHING

Self-Reflection Exercise #4 for Invalidate Others
Draw a picture of you (or you with others) in an occasion when you are invalidating others.

Awareness Exercises for Invalidate Others

Awareness of Body

a. Become aware of what your hands are doing when you are talking with someone. If you notice you are pointing at someone, drop your hand, continue talking, and notice how your body feels. Did the tone of what you were saying change?
b. Notice what your body posture is when you interrupt someone. How are you standing or leaning?
c. Become aware when you have lashed out and called someone a name or put someone down. Reflect on what you said by asking: How did my body feel when I said this? How did my body feel after I said this?
d. Notice your body posture and feelings when you are gossiping about someone. Contrast this with your body posture and feelings when you are talking about something positive.
e. Become aware of times when you clench your jaw, make a fist, curl your lip in anger, or raise your head to look down your nose. Begin to notice what you do with your face, hands, and the way you stand when you want control, feel threatened or want to be aggressive. For one week only, notice what others do with their body postures and facial expressions when they want control or are talking over or interrupting you (just observe them, do not comment).

Awareness of Thought and Speech

a. Use the shame log to record both spoken words and silent self-talk or thoughts. Take at least 10 days of these logs and examine any patterns you see that are Invalidate Others. If you need help finding a word look at the list of Shame Labels in the Appendix.
b. At the end of the day write down what you had nasty or judgmental thoughts about. What was occurring at the time?
c. Use the shame log to note how interactions are when you verbally attack, use a sarcastic or sharp comment, or say something to over-ride someone else's comments. Answer: Did this go well? Did we maintain a positive connection?

Awareness of Feelings

a. Twice a day, take a look at the Feeling Faces in the Appendix and identify how you are feeling. Use the list of Shame Labels in the Appendix to find a word if you need to. Record this for one or two weeks. Note how many times you identified you are angry, rage full, pissed off, upset, or mad at others.
b. Note if you feel ashamed after getting pissed off at someone. Write down what this feels like for you.
c. Answer: What feelings come up just before I mouth off about something or to someone?

Constellation #2
Invalidate Self

Our goal is to be seen as less than in relation to others. We believe we deserve contempt from others. We find ways to give our power away. We constantly disregard our own worth. We see ourselves as a victim.

Constellation #2
Invalidate Self

The way we relate to our unresolved shame in Invalidate Self is primarily through active self-loathing and self-hate. We truly *do not* believe that we are worthy just in and of ourselves. To make it more complex we sometimes do not know ourselves because we have "lived other people's lives" and not our own. This means we constantly defer to others' desires and preferences, pretending this is ok, not wanting to ruffle others' feathers.

Speaking up for ourselves while feeling unworthy and full of shame is difficult and awkward. We say "yes" to almost everything in order to avoid conflict or the fear of "losing" the other person. Saying "no" brings up huge fears of disapproval and abandonment by others. For this reason, it is difficult for us to set healthy boundaries with others. Establishing these boundaries would result in an opportunity to turn the focus toward ourselves. However, with the focus now turned toward ourselves we may feel selfish and slip into worrying "what others will think."

Invalidate Self can go so deep as to doubt that we have a right to exist because we believe that we do not count. If we believe we do not count, we will not feel worthy of asking for what we need or want. We hesitate to move forward with actions that require some risk and self-confidence.

Because of our belief that we are "not enough" we keep company with folks who confirm our conviction that we are unworthy. This validates the "less than" view we have of ourselves. We come across as needy and wanting and allow others to take advantage of us for their purposes. We believe if we are seen as helpful, kind, and giving perhaps someone will love us a bit. Since we do not like ourselves we depend on others' approval for our worth. We have little sense of self-approval.

Other aspects of Invalidate Self include consistently making light of oneself by engaging in self-ridicule (such as being the class clown or person who is always joking). This tactic might give ourselves some relief from not feeling good enough; after all we get people to laugh. However, this is not the laughter of enjoyment but a way to distract others from seeing inside us to our unresolved shame.

Other ways we keep people at a distance is to focus attention on something that is neutral, like the weather. This re-directs attention away from us. We can also get into a habit of being irrelevant and not staying on topic. We verbally wander all over the place, confusing and frustrating those who are trying to listen. The confusion acts like a wall or veil and protects us from being truly seen and heard. In addition to these tactics, we can become so absorbed about what we need to talk about – a kind of necessity to dump - that our interactions with others really become a continuous monologue. We stare blankly at others as they engage with us and when they have finished commenting or asking a question or two, we start right in again with our own topic without ever having acknowledged anything they said. Usually we don't really want to let them talk; we just want to rant on and on obsessively about whatever is eating at us. With all of these strategies others don't ever get a chance to know us very well – and that's the idea. Furthermore, we don't give ourselves a chance to get to know ourselves!

Another characteristic of Invalidate Self is to come across as befuddled and incapable. We believe we are incapable so we demonstrate this by being dumbfounded by the task at hand. This tactic gets others to feel sorry for us (because after all aren't we struggling?) and, we get to feed our self-pity by proving that we are at the mercy of our incompetence --- poor us we can't seem to do anything right. Often we inconvenience others or make their lives a bit more miserable because we just can't seem to get our act together.

Every strategy and tactic in Invalidate Others has to do with believing we are "not enough." We also show this by always apologizing for what we say or do. Internally we are sorry for being who we are. The constant "I'm sorry" is evidence of unresolved shame.

Invalidate Self is a mindset of believing that we deserve contempt. We put ourselves down before others get around to it using inner self-talk that is particularly self-loathing. We constantly remind ourselves that in the past we did terrible wrongs and that we will surely fail in the future. Our self-talk is a never ending string of harsh judgments. It is as if we cannot let ourselves believe that we are good enough by just being who we are. We often brush off our efforts to restore our dignity by taking a victim stance. Everyone and everything is against us and we wallow in self-pity followed by feelings of desperation and despair.

Real Life Stories

Story #1
An instructor relates a story about an adult learner in a class she taught. It was a small class of about seven people and the focus was on self-discovery and career choices. Over the course of two weeks each individual had been given a chance to share and discuss their life goals and difficulties reaching those goals. One evening the instructor took time with a student who had not shared very much. When the student was finished the student said, "I'm sorry I took so much time tonight." This response was typical of this student: saying they were sorry for many, many things and not allowing themselves the time that the instructor was happy to give to each student.

Story #2
Maria took a week to call her friend to tell her she could not go to the beach with her one Sunday. The trip had been planned in advance but Maria's life required her to pay attention to more important things such as finding new housing and looking for work while still tending to her family. Maria whined about the pain that came up for her around disappointing her friend by telling her she could not go. She had to be coached to learn to say it was just not a good time for her to go to the beach without over explaining her situation. The over explaining makes Maria sound like a victim of her circumstances.

Self-Reflection Exercises For Invalidate Self

In Invalidate Self our goal is to be seen as less than. We believe we deserve contempt from others. We habitually give our power away. We see ourselves as a victim.

Self-Reflection Exercise #1 for Invalidate Self
Below is a list of 14 behaviors used to Invalidate Self.

a) Put a check next to ones that you have used. Add some of your own.
b) On the next page, write about 2 occasions when you used any of the behaviors listed. Reflect on the outcome.

3. You put yourself down in a conversation so others won't take the chance to do it.
4. You are indecisive and do not bother to discover what you really want in any one situation. You often feel paralyzed, stuck, and afraid and therefore take no action.
5. Your self-talk is unkind. You often criticize, insult or degrade yourself.
6. You let others speak in demeaning ways to you, not saying anything while they do it in front of others. You never speak up about this.
7. You let your partner do demeaning sexual acts with you, even if you don't like it.
8. You fear being ridiculed or rejected if you ask for what you want. You do not speak up in an assertive manner to let others know how you feel or what you need.
9. When you pick out someone for a friend or relationship it is usually someone who does not treat you very well. You spend a lot of your time doing nice things for them seeking their approval. You do more nice things for them than you do for yourself.
10. Many people you choose to interact with never quite give you their full attention. Usually they talk about themselves. They are often self-centered people so transactions and interactions with them are on their terms.
11. You have come to believe you are a victim. You use language that refers to yourself as a "poor me." You whine and complain a lot. "I don't know why he does this to me." "I'm really not any good at this anyway." "They went behind my back."
12. You find fault with any suggestion to help change your situation for the better by using a "Ya but…" Nothing is ok the way it is, however you do nothing to change it. By keeping a pleasant manner about this others may feel sorry for you.
13. You either over groom or under groom. You care too much or not at all about public appearance. If others give you a compliment about yourself you shrug it off.
14. You make sure to never make anyone angry; therefore you will not confront the one whose actions are bothering you, although you may tell others. You get confused about how to confront in an assertive way.
15. You take extra care not to invade another person's space and are overly apologetic if you do.
16. You are overly apologetic and say "I'm sorry" constantly.

17. _____

18. _____

Occasion #1

Occasion #2

Self-Reflective Exercise #2 Invalidate Self

a) Describe a time when you felt like you did not "fit in." What did you tell yourself?

b) Describe a time when you let someone cross over a boundary with you. Perhaps you said "yes" to something that you know you needed to say "no" to, or you set aside your needs and let someone dictate what you "should do." Write about the outcomes of those situations.

c) Describe a time when you made light of something that you were truly upset about.

Self-Reflection Exercise #3 Invalidate Self

Looking at the list of behaviors for Invalidate Self, describe how you live your life as "the victim of circumstance." Include the <u>words</u> you tell yourself about yourself when your life doesn't go well.

_____

_____

_____

_____

_____

_____

_____

_____

_____

_____

_____

Self-Reflection Exercise #4 Invalidate Self
Using a drawing, show what invalidate self looks like to you.

Awareness Exercises for Invalidate Self

Awareness of Body

a. Notice when you cast your eyes downward when someone is speaking with you.
b. When you are putting yourself down either with what you are saying to yourself or openly in front of others, become aware of how you are standing or sitting. Where are your shoulders? Where are your hands? What sensation is occurring in your chest?
c. Take a week and notice when you feel distress. What part of your body hurts? Are you overly tired and doing a lot for others?
d. Ask: Is there a connection with how much you do for others and how much of a "victim" you feel?

Awareness of Thought and Speech

a. Using a simple log, record your self-talk every day for two weeks. Answer: Are these kind and hopeful comments to myself or self-put-downs? Do you shame yourself by using some of the words on the list of Shame Labels in the Appendix? Which ones occur most often?
b. Make an effort to change the words you say to yourself if they are unkind. Choose a few meaningful Shame Busting Statements from the appendix and start to use them.
c. Notice when you say I am sorry. Answer: Do you really want to say it, or is it done out of habit? Answer: Do I say I'm sorry frequently when it is really unnecessary?
d. Notice when you are over-explaining something to someone. Perhaps you have repeated the same thing over, but in a different way.

Awareness of Feelings

a. Twice a day look at the Feeling Faces in the Appendix and identify how you are feeling. Record this for one or two weeks. Note how many times you identified you are sad, fearful, shy, hesitant.
b. Note what feelings come up after you have interactions with people who you see as important to you (wife, husband, teachers, bosses, counselors etc.). Write down what feeling you believe you noticed.
c. Answer: What feelings come up just before I begin to interact with others that I see as authority figures or who I perceive as smarter than myself?
d. What feelings arise when I am alone? Consult the Feeling Faces in the Appendix. Also, use the list of Shame Labels in the Appendix if you need help identifying a feeling.

Constellation #3
Hide from Self

Our objective is to protect from our awareness any defect we believe we have. We distract ourself and others from seeing defects that may surface. We are often dishonest with ourself and others. We deceive and manipulate. We will do almost anything to stay in denial and often become addicted to drugs, alcohol, food, gambling, shopping, work or relationships.

Constellation #3
Hide from Self

Hide from Self is sometimes hard to get a handle on because denial is a large part of this strategy. If we are in denial we cannot see that we are hiding from our true inner self. We convince ourselves that our lies, deceits, and manipulations are really "our truth" and "besides we really didn't hurt anyone" or "what I do with my life is none of your business." Or, "all it may do is hurt me, and I'm ok with that." Or, "others do that, so what's the harm with me doing it?" This kind of talk is denial and the Hide from Self strategy does this well.

If we have fears of being seen and thought of as inadequate we learn to get very good at something and get people to focus on that. We are then well thought of by others in that particular area. This way we get people to notice where we are good at something and redirect their attention away from aspects of ourselves we find to be distasteful and undesirable. These parts that we deny without examination hold our unresolved shame.

If we are considered very handsome or beautiful or sexually appealing we can use these to our advantage. Or if we are very tall and big we can act tough, if we are short and small we can be quick with our words or be outrageous with our humor. These are ways we get others to avoid seeing any messiness we might have underneath the surface. We hide our self from our self. Deep inside we believe we are inadequate. However, we ignore this inadequacy by drawing attention to a trait that others find appealing, attractive, or fun.

Many of the actions and activities in the strategy of Hide from Self are socially acceptable. This makes it even more difficult to move out of denial. Drinking is often encouraged and socially acceptable. Even drug use can be encouraged in some circles. Owning expensive things and lots of them is seen as being successful and prosperous. We shop until we drop, brag about our sexual exploits, get stupid drunk, spend more than we have to stay in style and show everyone that we have "the latest," or we exercise obsessively to stay buff.

Hide from Self is all about showing the world "I am somebody." This is done with great effort on our part. On the inside, deep down, there is a core of worthlessness. Recognizing this core must be avoided at all costs. The unsaid rule of Hide from Self is "Never let them see you sweat." If anyone ever sees us "as we really are" it would be incredibly embarrassing and shameful. It would be so emotionally difficult that we might react with anger or rage in order to distance people. We have now moved into Invalidate Others in an attack mode. We might even get pissed off enough to destroy others or slide over to Invalidate Self and destroy ourselves.

The amount of internal pain that comes along with feeling worthless is so strong that we often want to drown it. So another part of Hide from Self is lots of drinking and drugging often to the point of addiction. When we do drugs and alcohol we do not feel our feelings. We temporarily keep away the pain of worthlessness. In addition, we have often become ashamed or frightened of our feelings. With our substance abuse we can stay numb and avoid feeling anything. Emotions give us clues to what is really going on inside us, but because we are in denial about what is going on inside it is best for us to make sure somehow we won't feel. Keeping super busy, running around doing things like a chicken with our head cut off, staying away from family by working too much are all ways we Hide from Self. Even traveling alot, or scheduling too much into the day or week is a way of keeping our selves away from our selves. If we sat down in the quiet and paid attention to our breath in meditation it would be extremely difficult – and maybe emotionally painful.

In Hide from Self is about oblivion. Oblivion means: staying in a daze and staying ignorant (as in uninformed). We stay in a stupor with drugs, alcohol, shopping, collecting stuff, feeling cool riding around in a BMW, or protected by a smoke-screen of other avoidance tactics. We come up with anything we can to stay dazed because if we come out of that daze we hit reality. And, reality is very uncomfortable and we don't like it. In Hide from Self, reality is often seen as boring and not entertaining enough because it is not exciting. Addiction to excitement and thrills not only shows others how daring we are but keeps us numb with adrenaline. The world is here to entertain us so that we can then become so distracted we ignore our imperfections. This is a disservice to our humanness and affects our bonds with others.

A Real Life Story
Latesha just had a fight with her boyfriend. She says to herself, "I'm no good at this relationship stuff. He is never going to love me. I blew it again." She starts to feel inadequate, incompetent, frustrated, despairing, and abandoned.

All of these feelings start to come up but Latesha pushes them down. Instead she begins to get a kind of sinking, heavy feeling in her chest. Then she quickly switches away from that and she finds herself becoming restless. She feels uncomfortable and a little edgy. The sensations increase in their level of discomfort. Latesha's mind switches thoughts and she finds herself thinking about the sweater she saw the last time she was shopping. She convinces herself that if she had a new look maybe she could attract a new guy; the "right" guy. So off she goes to Ross Dress for Less, determined to find that sweater that will give her that new look. Just the act of getting in the car creates both relief and excitement. The despair moves to the back seat of her awareness – for a while.

In this story the thinking about the sweater and the action of shopping is the magic potion of relief for the distress of the fight with the boyfriend that brought up Latesha's feelings of unworthiness – her unresolved shame.

Self-Reflection Exercises for Hide from Self

In Hide from Self your objective is to protect from awareness any possible defect. This is often done by manipulation and deceit with yourself and others. You distract yourself from facing any defects and you are often dishonest with others and yourself. You will do almost anything to stay in denial and often become addicted to drugs, alcohol, food, gambling, or shopping, relationships, etc.

Self-Reflection Exercise #1 for Hide from Self

Below is a list of 10 behaviors used to Hide from Self.

a) Put a check next to ones that you have used. Add some of your own.
b) On the next page write about 2 occasions when you used any of the behaviors listed. Reflect on the outcome.

1. You see yourself as a show-piece and only show others part of yourself. Anything real about you is kept "under wraps." You want life to be like a movie.
2. You must look "very good" *all* the time. You have the latest fashions and name brands.
3. You stay very, very busy. Every minute of every day is planned. There is no tolerance for down time.
4. You are obsessed about work. You think about it and talk about it when you are not at work. When someone asks you how you are you must include what you are doing at work. You like to impress others about your work. You are your work.
5. In conversations you often lie, exaggerate, or keep the conversation off-balance by being irrelevant. You use charm to get the other person to talk about themselves. Others may say you have a "swelled head."
6. You usually have had many lovers. You believe you cannot live without sex. You try to score anywhere you are. You become very good at all phases of the sexual encounter. You see others as sexual objects that are there for you to "conquer" and have a sexual experience with.
7. You are narcissistic: The definition of narcissistic from Random House dictionary, p. 885 is: "Gratification derived from admiration of one's own physical or mental attributes."
8. You indulge in any behavior that is hedonistic, meaning --wild and pleasure-seeking. You go for any event that produces a lot of excitement and gives you a "rush."
9. You cannot go without drugs, alcohol, or gambling. You choose to stay high and unaware of any of your feelings and your defects. You feel odd when *not* using an addictive substance.
10. You look for admiration from others for your dangerous or wild conduct.

11. _____
    _____
    _____

12. _____
    _____
    _____

Occasion#1

Occasion #2

Self-Reflection Exercise #2 Hide from Self

a) Describe how you have either been somehow deceitful, not told the whole truth or out-right lied to someone in the past 2 months. Write about a time you may have misled someone with fanciful words. Reflect on how you may have affected the other person.

_____

_____

_____

_____

_____

b) Describe what you do to "keep in style" – hair do's, clothing, shoes, etc. Examine how often you shop for the current styles and perhaps spend beyond your means. Describe how you feel and what you do when your "image" isn't "up to par" on certain days.

_____

_____

_____

_____

_____

c) List the ways you try to stay "out of it" or keep your feelings at a distance either through drug use, drinking, over-working, over-eating or keeping "on-the-go."

_____

_____

_____

_____

_____

Self-Reflection Exercise #3 Hide from Self
With as much self-examination as possible list 10 reasons you don't want people to see "the real you."

1._____

2._____

3._____

4._____

5._____

6._____

7._____

8._____

9._____

10._____

Self-Reflection Exercise #4 Hide from Self

Either draw a *representation* of the perfect you or find a picture in a magazine that resembles your "*perfect you*" image. Discuss your drawing or your picture choice with someone you can talk openly with and are willing to receive input from.

Awareness Exercises for Hide from Self

Awareness of Body

a. Become aware when you have a craving – a strong longing. It can be a craving for your food, alcohol or a drug, a desire for sex or for a flirtatious encounter (you must have him! Or you must see her!), a "got to have that" purchase, or even as small as you "must have a cup of coffee." Ask: What does my body feel like now when I am craving something? What sensations are occurring as I try to satisfy this craving? What does my body feel like after I have satisfied the craving?
b. Become aware when someone questions or complains about your drinking or drug use. What reaction does your body have when someone mentions their concern or annoyance about your drinking or drug use?
c. Begin to become aware when emotional pain arises. For example, you may start thinking about an ex-girlfriend or boyfriend. If emotional pain comes up – such as hurt, anger, sadness, or general heartache, *notice what you do to avoid feeling this pain*. Keep a log of what you notice.
d. What sensations occur in your body when you are exaggerating?
e. Notice how your body feels when you are talking about exciting events or drinking and drugging. Notice if you brag.

Awareness of Thought and Speech

a. Begin to notice when you start to exaggerate when talking with someone. Notice what words you use to build up excitement, to make someone or something bigger and better than it actually is.
b. Begin to notice when you tell lies or fibs. During what circumstances do you lie or fib? How does your body feel after you tell a fib?
c. Notice how often you talk about drinking, drugging or events that give an adrenaline rush (like car racing, skiing, etc.)

Awareness of Feelings

a. Using the Feeling Faces identify one feeling every day. Name it and write it down for 2 weeks. At the end of 2 weeks see which feeling was repeated the most, the second most. Use the list of Shame Labels for additional help if needed.
b. Take your feeling log from above and choose a feeling. Write a sentence or two about where the feeling occurs in your body and what your body feels like.
c. Keep a daily log for 2 weeks on the sensation of craving. You may include time of the craving, what you are craving, and what you do about the craving. Answer: Does craving get less at the end of the 2-week log

Constellation #4
Hide from Others

Our goal is to not have our inner self exposed for others to see because we are ashamed of our "self." The way this is managed is by isolating. We choose to have limited connection with others. We lead a "smaller" life because we hide yourself away for fear of what others may think.

Constellation #4
Hide from Others

Hide from Others handles unresolved shame by retreating and withdrawing. The idea is to hide and keep ourselves away from others. We do this because we do not feel ok or good enough, competent enough, or that we truly fit in and belong. Interaction with others feels dangerous because it requires, on some level, that we let somebody see even the smallest part of ourselves and that feels unsafe. We only show a bit of ourselves in public or in a group. We stay with generalizations, not revealing details about our life experience because someone may take that information to use against us at some time.

The result of the actions of Hide from Others is lost connections. We find ways to maintain a distance with family, co-workers, "friends," neighbors, and the world in general. Without these connections we are left in our own little world, free to think, feel and make-up our own rules and of life. We have practiced not letting others know what we are feeling and thinking. This means we might keep silence, say as few words as necessary in an interaction, and maintain a "stone face" that doesn't show an emotion. We may try very hard not to look anyone in the eye. Examples of acting out Hide from Others are the quiet neighbor who doesn't bother anyone and just says hello, or the "strong, silent type" for guys or the very modest, shy woman.

The Hide from Others strategy can provide a sense of safety as we choose to remove ourselves from a shameful event. Sometimes we need to re-group for a while and then return to being social with others after having recovered enough. Society says that it is ok if we withdraw a bit as appropriate if something is embarrassing. An example of this might be spilling something in public and retreating to the restroom to clean up and then returning.

It is important to understand that in Hide from Others there is a range of withdrawal. At the low end of the range we may get very quiet about a personal matter of shame and withhold sharing with someone. Inside we fear that someone will discover we are incapable, faulty, inadequate, or "not good enough." We may think this protecting ourselves, but often the shame remains with us and we end up carrying it around in a sack, never setting it down, and never opening it up to look inside. The sack becomes awkward and clumsy to carry getting in the way of our full participation in life's challenges and joys. On the other end of the range we isolate ourselves from others ninety percent of any day or week. People might refer to us as a recluse or weird or unfriendly.

We may be the quiet neighbor next door that you never see. We stay to ourselves, watch a lot of TV, play video games, read, keep the ear pieces in from the iPod and listen to music, etc. We limit our actions to anything that does not require engaging and connecting with other people. This then, limits our exposure and we feel more secure. We don't bother to be part of our neighborhood or community.

In Hide from Others we often believe that even if we contribute and participate it would be insufficient. Therefore, in order to avoid feeling a sense of deficiency that is painful, we limit ourselves, hide, and create our own worlds in which to live safely. We remove ourselves from the scenes and situations that triggered our shame. This keeps us safe, but diminishes our life and allows us only a narrow windowed view of the world.

A Real Life Story

Fred would not let anyone in the neighborhood shovel the snow on the sidewalk in front of his house. The rest of the people on the street had pitched in and helped each other but Fred got upset when others "interfered." He continued to limit his interaction with neighbors and kept to himself as much as possible refusing invitations to join neighborhood gatherings and dinner invitations. Often a friend of his would have to call the police to check on him because he would not answer his phone, and being diabetic, his friend had concerns.

Self-Reflection Exercises for Hide from Others

In Hide from Other you restrict your interactions with others.
Your withdrawal lessens the quality of our life.

Self-Reflection Exercise #1 for Hide from Others
Below is a list of 9 behaviors used to Hide from Others.

   a) Put a check next to ones that you use. Add some of your own.
   b) On the next page write about 2 occasions when you used any of the behaviors listed. Reflect on the outcome.

1. You choose to isolate and separate yourself from others. You do not reach out to others for company or help. When you go to visit friends or family you put yourself in front of the TV.
2. You are the silent, shy type. You do not participate when in a group. Up speak when spoken to but not much beyond that. You believe that you do not really have very much to offer.
3. You sleep too much (all weekend or every chance you can get).
4. You have a great deal of fear of being noticed. You remove yourself from interactions. You space out – perhaps looking off into the distance – when others are speaking about something.
5. You do not mix with people and prefer to be alone. People would say about you: "He keeps to himself a lot."
6. You are not interested in reaching out to make meaningful connections with others.
7. You stay at home and watch TV or play video games rather than go to AA or NA meetings. If you do go you sit in the back, not talk to anyone there and leave early.
8. You do not talk with others if you have a problem. You try work things out on your own.
9. Sharing or speaking in a group makes you extremely self-conscious and fearful. Your heart pounds, your face can get red, and you often speak very softly.

10. _____
    _____
    _____
    _____

11. _____
    _____
    _____
    _____

12. _____
    _____
    _____
    _____

JANE R. PENNINGTON M.A.

Occasion#1

SHAME: SHOULD HAVE ALREADY MASTERED EVERYTHING

Occasion#2

Self-Reflection Exercise #2 Hide from Others

a) Write about a time when you limited your interactions with others because you felt self-conscious.

_____
_____
_____
_____
_____
_____

b) Describe a time when you chose not to reach out to others even though you would have likely benefited somehow by doing so.

_____
_____
_____
_____
_____
_____

Self-Reflection Exercise #3 Hide from Others

a) Name 10 ways you choose to isolate and avoid others.

1. _____
2. _____
3. _____
4. _____
5. _____
6. _____
7. _____
8. _____
9. _____
10. _____

b) Reflect how this choice to isolate and avoid has affected the quality and manner of your life.

_____
_____
_____
_____
_____

Self-Reflection Exercise #4 Hide from Others
Make 3 drawings. (Note: Make sure to label who the people are in the drawings.)

a) In the first drawing indicate a figure that is you in a room with several other people (label them family, acquaintances friends, etc.). Place yourself a distance from them that is most comfortable for you. Indicate how much time you are willing to spend with them.

b) In the second drawing indicate a figure that is you in a situation with a person you have just met. Place yourself a distance from them that is most comfortable for you. Indicate how much time you are willing to spend with them.

c) In the third drawing indicated a figure that is you with someone with whom you would like to get to know better. Place yourself a distance from them that is most comfortable for you. Indicate how much time you are willing to spend with them.

Self-Reflection Exercise #5 Hide from Others
Draw a picture of yourself in relationship with all the other people in your life.

Awareness Exercises for Hide from Others

Awareness of Body

a. Begin to notice how your body feels when you choose not to engage with others in conversation or participate in a group activity.
b. Notice how your body feels when you have a problem and choose to remain quiet about it rather than discuss it with anyone. Is there a tightness anywhere in your body?
c. When you are asked to speak in a class or a meeting immediately notice how your body responds to this request. Notice also how you feel as you speak.
d. After spending time interacting with people, notice how your body feels. Contrast this with noticing how your body feels when you are alone.

Awareness of Thought and Speech

a. Using a simple log keep a list of words you notice you use to keep other people away. (Examples might include: "No."; "Excuse me."; "Sorry, I need to go.")
b. Start noticing your self-talk. Keep a simple log of your self-talk (this is inner dialogue). (Examples are: "Get me out of here." "I wish I could hide." "I want to run away." "Talking with this person is really uncomfortable").
c. Notice when you do not join in with a conversation and stay on the side, being quiet, trying not to be noticed.

Awareness of Feelings

a. Using the Feeling Faces in the Appendix chart identify one feeling you have every day. Keep a chart. Which feeling occurs most often? If you need more help identifying feelings look at the list of Shame Labels in the Appendix.
b. Note what feelings come up before and after you interact with someone or a group of people. Write the feelings down and look at your notes once a week. What patterns do you notice? Use the list of Shame Labels if you need more help identifying feelings.
c. Take your feeling log from above and choose a feeling. Write a sentence or two about your experience of this feeling. Examine whether you hate the feeling and really want to avoid it. Ask: Is there a connection between wanting to avoid the feeling and staying away from others to keep the feeling away.

Part Two

As shame is resolved through your awareness and acknowledgment you become more capable of practicing being your Wise-Self.

Being Your Wise-Self is a Process

Being Your Wise-Self

As we can see by the drawing for this part of the workbook being our Wise-Self is a process. We start slowly, sometimes stumbling along the way. The process of uncovering your Wise-Self is the process of learning how to drop our self-protective strategies, and over time, build the capacity to respond differently. Our Wise-Self responses mean that we are more vulnerable and by being this way we show more of who we really are. We end bullying, judging, and criticizing our way through life and become humble. A Wise-Self is their "right-size", no longer bigger and more than others, or smaller and less than others.

It does not mean that others walk all over us. Instead, we practice sticking up for ourselves in more wholesome (not necessarily perfect) ways and come to see that the results are more rewarding. We become more capable of accessing a centering place inside. We let difficult feelings arise and have less chance of being sucked into a vortex that carries us away as Dorothy in the Wizard of Oz was carried away in the tornado.

Being aware is still key in moving towards being our Wise-Self. By observing ourselves we learn about the process – the road map of our reactions and responses. Even in the middle of a self-protective and defensive reaction the ability to observe what we are saying, doing, and feeling is a huge gift. Observing ourselves "in-the-act" brings us information and with that information we learn to detect what needs to change in order to practice being our Wise-Self.

As we observe and learn about ourselves we recognize that we can develop, nurture, and cultivate new ways of responding. We may notice we are moving into a defense strategy, then stop, and consciously choose a Wise-Self response. Or, we may do a whole, brand new way of being and acting, stepping into being our Wise-Self completely and confidently the very first time we decide to respond a new way. Either way, like everything that is new to us, being our Wise-Self requires practice.

On p. 70 there are four ways of being your Wise-Self followed by two true stories of real people practicing their Wise-Self in situations. Read these carefully and then begin to "change your emotional karma" (as Kevin Griffin suggests) by doing the beginning self-reflection exercises on p. 75. It's worth the effort!

Four Ways of Being Your Wise-Self

For each set of strategies we use to self-protect and defend against our unresolved shame there is a corresponding set of strategies that is non-defensive and wholesome. To practice wholesome ways of being means to have skillful, thoughtful responses with others and a capacity to nurture oneself. These strategies result in connected, loving and balanced relationships with less drama, more self-confidence, and a more satisfying relationship with others and yourself.

Respect Others
Here we have regard for others. We become willing to let go of having power and control. The focus changes from being about us --- our agenda --- to genuine interest in others. We become willing to recognize where others are at in this particular moment and meet them where *they* are. We become open to hearing others opinions and views, no matter how difficult it is for us to be quiet and listen.

Respect Self
Here we feel vital and alive. We express strength. We know that what we do and say counts in this world. We stick up for ourselves by learning to speak our truth in an assertive way. We think positive thoughts and take positive action to nurture and care for ourselves. We stop selling ourselves short.

Present with Self
Here we have integrity with ourselves. We stay real. We are aware of how we feel at any one moment and use that as information to guide and regulate our behaviors. We choose to stay away from numbing behaviors and substances. We examine our part in difficult transactions with others, we maintain our honesty at all times, and we get our needs met by being assertive and forthright.

Present with Others
Here we participate in our relationships, both personal and in the community. We contribute what we can and sometimes stretch ourselves to get involved in a positive way even when we would rather hide. We begin to believe that our contribution has value.

Examples of Practicing Being Your Wise-Self

Steve's story of being his Wise-Self
One day my partner and I were getting ready to make breakfast together. In the course of the conversation before-hand she said something to me that felt very shaming. It was about working. This is a sensitive area for me. I immediately noticed that I felt inadequate and incompetent, bad, and wrong. I also noticed that I wanted to blame her for these feelings I was having. I noticed that my chest felt tight and hurt and that my breathing had shortened. These are all of my responses when I am dealing with my shame wound.

I stood there looking at her while I was noticing all that was going inside me. I began to sense I needed some time and space. I realized that I needed to discontinue the conversation. I stated that I was having some strong feelings and that I needed to go out of the house and sit outside for a few minutes and I would return shortly. I said this politely and calmly.

I wanted to give myself a place to manage what was arising and to do this alone, away from my partner. I left the house and went in the back yard under the apple tree and sat in a chair. I closed my eyes and gently focused on how my body felt. I focused on the in-and-out breath and just sat. I didn't try to "think it through." I sat and let whatever came up for me come up and observed it.

What I observed was that I was the one that had labeled myself shamed by the comment. My partner just said what she thought she needed to say. It was her opinion. It still could have been a shaming comment (meant to put me in my place and make her feel better – Invalidate Others) but I was the one that picked up the comment and then labeled it shame. Once I saw this (it was amazingly clear) I let go of the label. I understood that I could take that label off easily because I had been the one to put the label on. Following this understanding and realization, I stopped taking her comment to heart (personally) and I let go of any blame on her. I felt lighter and my chest felt less constricted.

I walked back in the house and said to her that I felt ok now and was ready to make breakfast. We didn't analyze anything. I didn't share anything except that I felt better. I became present with her, focusing on the present moment and not picking apart the past or what she said. I had resolved the unresolved shame and was then able to have a loving morning of having breakfast together. We had a pleasant day. This is peace.

Now, I'll share what I know, in my heart of hearts, would have happened years ago without having done any shame wound work. I would have screamed something awful at her – put her down hurtfully. This means I would have moved immediately into Invalidate Others to avoid feeling and observing what was arising in me. Then I would have thrown something and stomped out the door, got in the car and found a place to go (maybe a bar? Hide from Self) and stewed. I would have felt guilty after a while. I would have crawled back and made an awkward attempt at forgiveness. I would have ruined the entire day and felt awful (Invalidate Self) for days later. This is drama.

That's an example of practicing noticing in order to become your Wise-Self. In this example, I could sense very strongly, that I wanted to move into Invalidate Self and Invalidate Others. However, I chose to observe – look – stay with what was arising in me and witness it. If I had gotten sucked into the vortex I would have screamed and yelled at my partner.

Understanding Steve's story as a Way of Being Your Wise-Self
In the example above it must be remembered that Steve had to become willing to notice what was going on inside him. This means he could not let himself get swept up by his feelings of shame and react to defend them. He had to "stand back" and notice them and then choose an action that created some emotional space (being outside alone). Perhaps in another situation or with a topic other than work, what his partner said to him would not have had such a strong impact. Recognizing and noticing the beginning signals of a strong reaction made a huge difference in the nature of his response.

Sue's Experience of Being her Wise-Self
A friend of mine really likes to take control of situations and tell people what they need to do, especially if they are interfering with her way of doing things. She has called herself a bully, forceful, aggressive and pushy. In an attempt to correct and change some of this behavior she is practicing being more her Wise-Self. This is how she did it:

While at a music concert enjoying a very popular group and having paid a lot of money for the seats she noticed some folks smoking even though the area was designated as non-smoking. Instead of being in their face about it she called over an usher for the event and asked him if he would please say something to the smokers. She did this politely. He said he was happy to do so and thanked her for bringing it to his attention. He asked the people to honor the non-smoking designation and everything went on smoothly.

The second thing that happened at the concert were some people seated behind her drinking a lot and being very loud and disorderly. She turned around to them and smiled and introduced herself and her husband to them and learned their names. They chatted for a few minutes about how great it was to be able to see the group perform live and how much they both enjoyed the group's music. The loud couple were respectful and quiet for the rest of the performance.

Understanding Sue's Story as a Way of Being Your Wise-Self

First, by choosing to hand over control to the usher Sue let go of trying to have all the power and control over others. She reached out and asked for help with a situation, realizing that she could try and get her need (to stop smoking) met through the action of someone other than herself. She let go of having to have power and control and actually used the correct authority that was assigned the power and control of maintaining the rules of the concert.

Second, by choosing to connect with the noisy drinkers behind her with a smile and conversation about the concert they both wanted to enjoy, she met them equally. She did not force her agenda by scolding them about their behavior. She humanized them. She got what she wanted by being her Wise-Self and not being bigger than them (I'm a good concert-goer, I'm courteous and you're not.) She didn't even have to ask for less ruckus and noise so she could enjoy the group's music! Treating people and connecting with them as fellow concert goers (finding the common ground) and reaching out with a smile instead of a snarl made this a peaceful and enjoyable experience.

Summary

Doing what is necessary in a kind and caring manner to manage the impact maintains peace in ourselves and with others. When we act out because of the impact there is no peace. If we can learn to tolerate the discomfort and *not* defend against what arises in us, we give ourselves the space to choose to take action that is responsible and caring.

These new ways of acting and thinking do not come easily and again we must practice and then practice more. However, if we know what to reach for instead of our defenses it will become easier to stop grabbing a defensive strategy. Our defenses can often be ingrained in us –they can be very automatic. We are using them before we even know we are using them. Being our Wise-Self can become automatic too. It just takes practice!

Working with being your Wise-Self

In the next few pages this is what you will find:

1) A set of Beginning Self-Reflection Exercises
2) A two to three page description of each way of being your Wise-Self with a A Real Life Story for each
3) A set of Self-Reflection Exercises for each Wise-Self way
4) A list of Practices for using your Wise-Self
5) Awareness Exercises for your Wise-Self

Suggestions on how to use Part Two

1) Read pages 69 to 72 to get the over-all idea of being your wise-self. Then do the Beginning Self-Reflection Exercises on pages 75 to 79 as a warm-up.
2) Take time to read each Wise-Self description.
3) Give yourself some quiet space and time to do the Self-Reflection Exercises.
4) Start right in with the Awareness Exercises. They will help you to begin to do life differently and to increase your self-awareness. There may be some wonderful positive rewards too!
5) Begin using the lists of Practices for being your Wise Self a little at a time. Pick something you have confidence you can practice. Log them or share them with someone you trust.

   a. Use one Wise-Self Practice (one line at a time), for a half day, one day or one week (however long you choose).
   b. You may use one page as an inventory for one day, one week, or one month and examine how you did at the end of your chosen time period.

Beginning Self-Reflection Exercises for Being Your Wise-Self

"While most of us develop habitual ways of thinking and feeling….it is possible at any time to incline the mind differently. This is how we change our emotional karma."

A Burning Desire: Dharma God & The Path of Recovery by Kevin Griffin

Beginning Self-Reflection Exercise #1

Read the Being Your Wise- Self Introduction and the Examples of Practicing Being Your Wise-Self then immediately upon finishing, write or draw what being your Wise-Self means for you.

Beginning Self-Reflection Exercise #2

The four ways of being your Wise-Self are summarized below. Write down some ideas of how to use each one in your current life situation.

Respect Others: Regard

Here we have regard for others. We become willing to let go of having power and control. The focus changes from being about us --- our agenda --- to genuine interest in others. We become willing to recognize where others are at in this particular moment and meet them where *they* are. We become open to hearing others opinions and views, no matter how difficult it is for us to be quiet and listen.

_____

_____

Respect Self: Vitality & Liveliness

Here we feel vital and alive. We express vitality. We know that what we do and say counts in this world. We stick up for ourselves by learning to speak our truth in an assertive way. We think positive thoughts and take positive action to nurture and care for ourself.

_____

_____

Present with Self: Integrity

Here we are aware of how we feel at any one moment and use that as information to guide and regulate our behaviors. We choose to stay away from numbing behaviors and substances. We examine our part in difficult transactions with others, we maintain our honesty at all times, and we get our needs met by being assertive and forthright.

_____

_____

Present with Others: Participation

Here we participate in our relationships, both personal and in the community. We contribute what we can and sometimes stretch ourselves to get involved in a positive way even when we would rather hide. We begin to believe that our contribution has value.

_____

_____

Beginning Self-Reflection Exercise #3

Part 1: Taking your answers from Self-Reflection Exercise #2 reflect on what barriers you might have in following through with your Wise-Self actions. Some suggestions about types of barriers would be: fear of change and doing things differently, other people's opinions and reactions if you do change, emotional blocks such as anger, depression, or shyness. What are your barriers?

_____

_____

_____

_____

_____

_____

Part 2: List 5 to 10 ways you could start to practice overcoming the barriers you wrote about in Part 1

1.

2.

3.

4.

5.

Respect Others

Here we have regard for others. We become willing to let go of having power and control. The focus changes from being about us --- our agenda --- to genuine interest in others. We become willing to recognize where others are at in this particular moment and meet them where *they* are We become open to hearing others' opinions and views, no matter how difficult it is for to listen.

Respect Others

Respect Others has far-reaching implications. Respecting Others includes all kinds of relationships whether they are close relationships or strangers we speak with during our daily routines. Respect Others also includes showing reverence and regard to those in our neighborhood and, the community at large, including respect and regard for our physical surroundings, no matter what kind of space we are currently living in.

Respect Others requires a shift in focus, from our agenda, to consideration of the needs and wants of others. Sometimes it will be necessary to let go of our needs and wants and go with what is beneficial for the group. The "group" may mean our 12 Step group, our immediate family, our spouse, our extended family, and their friends (such as friends of our son or daughter).

This does not mean that we are constantly bowing to others actions or opinions. It does mean that we suspend or hold-off coming "at" others no matter how much we have been triggered. It means that we recognize we have been triggered and we work with that trigger so that we refrain from discharging undeserved accusations, hurt, anger, and shame on to others. These are ours and we must say "I own this" instead of laying it on others. When we choose to own, or refrain and keep our opinions and reactions to ourselves, then we have begun to Respect Others.

Respect Others has to do with choosing to give the other person or group enough room to express themselves. No matter how much we disagree we set aside our opinions and give our time to listen. Sometimes it's fun to just practice this on purpose. Once during a presidential campaign I chose to ask a few people that I ran into who they were voting for and when they would say the opposite of my candidate (I didn't let them know) I would purposely listen (and calmly ask questions) to what they had to say about "the other candidate." I would just listen, not agreeing or disagreeing and not engaging in any disproving, or countering anything. I got to learn how others think. It was very enlightening!

However, it is not only when we are listening that we must keep ourselves in check. Sometimes when we are talking about something charged with emotion for us we don't want to let others comment. We may be so anxious to get our point across and show others "how right we are" that we end up pushing our agenda onto others. Respect Others asks that we refrain from forcing and trying to get others to see things our way.

If someone calls us a name or yells at us or you think they look at us "the wrong way," Respect Others asks that we manage our reaction to this internally and not move rapidly into a "come back" that puts the other in their place or puts them down. In Respect Others we notice when we have jumped to conclusions about others or have made an assumption. We can then practice asking others what is true for them, what they need, or want. We may not like the answer, but then we get a chance to practice acceptance (of what we cannot change) and apply the process of changing what we can (usually our attitude).

Some people might interpret the strategy of Respect Others as giving away ones' power. But this is not true. What we are doing when we Respect Others is maintaining power and control over *ourself*, as well as we can in that one particular moment. The idea is to practice keeping the focus on ourself with careful awareness of what is arising in us. No one is going to be perfect at this all the time. However, if we can start to notice a slight change in a less aggressive direction or in small increments in doing things more gently then we are on our way.

For example, blurting out that we felt hurt by someone's actions or words is a huge difference (and has more power) than blurting out a sarcastic put down.

When we manage our reactions from within, we have the focus in the right place. Since Invalidate Others is often about discharging our shame on to others, Respect Others is learning how *not* to discharge our shame on to others. It is practicing "staying with" whatever negative and strong reactions come up. This refraining from and then, observing your inner state, is using our internal power and resources rather than focusing outward to have power over others.

Respect Others means that you let go of trying to control situations and stop having to have things our way. We stop the one-ups-man-ship and drop our sense of self-importance and superiority. We become willing to be open to others' views and we become genuinely interested in what they have to say. For a time, we put aside our opinions. And, then later, we ask if the others in the interaction want our opinions or advice. When we do speak we keep positive and refrain from saying anything that may harm.

Real Life Stories

A teacher and group facilitator relates this story:
One day as I was teaching a life-skills class and I wanted to make sure that a certain group of students in the class not only understood what I was trying to get across but that they knew that what we were discussing was "the right and better way" to do things, after all their way had not been working for a long time. I found myself standing next to the table they were sitting at and saw my hand extended toward them with my finger pointing at them. When I became aware of my body language, I stopped pointing, brought my arm down to my side and lowered my voice and then made sure to take time to listen to what they had to say.

Pedro's response during a driving incident:
I pulled onto a curving road (the visibility was very poor) and another driver had to jam on his brakes. I thought he may have been driving too fast, but I focused on whether he was ok. We got out of our cars. He was angry and came toward me and pushed me. I stayed self-contained and observed the situation. I felt a powerful, positive energy from him. I respect him and myself for not adding to the upset.

An experience observed while working in a rehabilitation program at a prison:
One day one of residents came over to me even though he was not on my counselor case load. Paul reported that he had another resident be rather verbally aggressive and pushy with him. This had been a repetitive pattern for Harry to do this with Paul. Paul usually ended up engaging in argumentative conversation with Harry who always seemed to "push Paul's buttons." But this time Paul happily reported that he had just listened to Harry and did not engage with him. Paul said he waited the day out and later went to Harry to talk. This was new behavior for Paul. In addition Paul reported that he was able to have some compassion for Harry by putting himself in Harry's shoes

Paul was thrilled to report about how he had noticed how he refrained from attacking Harry back. Paul had also consciously decided to give some room to just let Harry express himself. Paul reported that later in the day when neither of them were "all fired-up" but calmer, they were able to discuss things as equals, not as two aggressive individuals trying to "lord it over" each other. Paul now believed that his relationship with Harry would improve.

Self-Reflection Exercise #1 for Respect Others

1. Write about ways you can refrain and use self-control in practicing Respect Others. Describe how this might affect your communication with someone.

_____

_____

_____

_____

_____

_____

_____

Self-Reflection Exercise #2 for Respect Others

Describe three interactions with others where you wanted to be aggressive but chose to be assertive instead. Reflect: In what ways is assertive different for you than aggressive? How did you feel afterward? What was the outcome of the interaction?

1.

2.

3.

Self-Reflection Exercise #3 for Respect Others

Starting with 1 minute, then increasing to 2 minutes, then 5 minutes, then 20 to 30 minutes, do a loving-kindness meditation.

Instructions: Sitting in a quiet place, no shoes, feet on floor, hands placed on top of legs, straight but relaxed and supported back, and close your eyes:

1) Bring to your mind someone who is important to you, someone you like and respect. See them happy and smiling.
   Repeat to yourself:

   May you be well.
   May you be happy.
   May you abide in peace.
   May you feel safe and secure.
   May you feel loved and cared for.

2) Bring to mind someone you got irritated/upset with today. Repeat the above meditation several times.
3) Bring to mind someone who has hurt you and are concerned about seeing or meeting in the future. Repeat the above meditation several times.
4) *If you're really into this*: Bring to mind someone or a group of people you have discovered you have distaste for. Repeat the above meditation several times.

After repeating the words silently to yourself several times you may choose to sit and focus on your breathing or any other body sensations that arise. Just go back to your breath if you start thinking or day-dreaming. Then, before you leave your chair, choose a person or group to bring to mind as suggested above and repeat the words of the loving-kindness meditation.

JANE R. PENNINGTON M.A.

Self-Reflection Exercise #4 for Respect Others
Draw how you would look, your facial expression, your body language, when you are making an effort to Respect Others. You may include other figures in your drawing perhaps showing how you relate to specific people in your life when you are respecting them.

Awareness Exercises for Respect Others

Awareness of Body

a. Become aware of how you are standing when you are listening intently. Where are your eyes focused? How is your posture? What are your hands doing?
b. How do you show others respect with your body posture, facial expressions, and hand gestures?
c. Describe what you sense in your body when you have had a good exchange with someone.

Awareness of Thought and Speech

a. Using a log or note book record the thoughtful and respectful words you use with others at work, home, and in the community. Do this for one week. Did your use of respectful words increase by the end of the week? What were some outcomes?
b. Keep a log using these questions to track your speech.
   - Did I pick the right time to tell someone something difficult?
   - Was it truthful?
   - Was it spoken affectionately?
   - Was it beneficial?
   - Were my intentions for good?
c. Answer: Did I refrain from ill-speech (putting other's down, gossip) one day at a time? One hour at a time? Keep a log of what situations or people are harder to practice kind speech with.

Awareness of Feelings

a. Using the Feeling Faces Appendix, identify 3 positive feelings that occur as you interact with people in a day. What kind of pattern do you see? What can you do to increase the occurrence of more positive feelings in a month?
b. Make a conscious effort to shift your focus to discovering what you are feeling during the day. Check in with yourself at least 3 times a day. Make a note about the feeling when you do this.
c. Answer: What kind of feelings can I access to help me stay centered and listening respectfully when someone is expressing an opinion you are uncomfortable with?

Practices for Respect Others

Start practicing these as often as possible. You can start with one or several or all of them. Keep an inventory when practicing and check daily or weekly to see how it's going.

1. I put aside my opinion and listen with interest to a different opinion.

2. I choose kind, thoughtful and respectful words when speaking at work, home, and to those in public.

3. When a difficult or conflicted situation arises I keep the focus on myself and my part in it and *did not* immediately look for fault in things or people outside myself.

4. I realize that that I did not have all the answers and did not force my reasoning and thinking on others.

5. I chose to *not* put others down in order to feel better about myself.

6. I present myself to others as an equal, no less than others, no better than others.

7. I keep the focus on myself and realize that I cannot really know how another feels.

8. I refrain from gossip about others.

9. I am capable of letting others see some of my vulnerabilities.

10. I practice not guessing other's motives for doing things. I ask them and I believe their response.

Respect Self

Here we feel vital and alive. We express vitality. We know that what we do and say counts in this world. We stick up for ourselves by learning to speak our truth in an assertive way. We think uplifting and positive thoughts, shifting from the negative. We take positive action to nurture and care for ourselves.

Respect Self

Respect Self is all about starting to believe in our own self-worth. In order to do this we first must take up the task of discovering how we feed our negativity, then gradually let go of what is harmful to ourselves and replacing it with the practice of honoring our self in all areas of our life. It is highly recommended that in order to become vital and alive more positive and healthy attitudes about ourselves be developed. We must put into practice, actions, thoughts, and feelings that advance our well-being and contribute to gaining our personal power. The key to doing this is to *do it* through the practices out lined in this section.

Gaining our personal power means taking responsibility and ownership. We consciously leave the "pity party." We can simply start by changing a few of the words we use when talking about a situation. We can change "you" to "I" and when speaking about a situation focus on how it affects us and specifically name what we don't like and ask for what we want. For example, instead of "Don't *you* know what kind of mess *you* cause when *you* are late?!" we can say, "*I* feel disregarded and hurt when you said you would come at six and you are here at seven. Please be here at six next time." We can also change "they" to "I". For example, you might say: "*They* never get this paper work right!" but we change it to: "*I* wonder what I can do differently to make sure the paper work is right? Who could *I* contact to help straighten this out?" This kind of communication helps us keep the focus on ourselves and helps us stop pointing outward which in turn moves us out of the "victim hood"!

The sentences in the previous paragraph use "I" statements. Using "I" statements is a big part of Respect Self because they are assertive. In Respect Self as we start to become more assertive in our interactions we begin to create a more secure and confident self.

In Respect Self we begin to practice treating ourselves with value by learning how to "fill ourselves up" rather than asking others to do this for us. In addition, as we practice being there for ourselves, we stop trying to get *all* of our needs met by others. We also practice developing relationships with healthy people and get our needs met in a variety of healthy ways.

When we are practicing Respect Self if someone tells us what they think is best for us to do or how to act in a particular situation, we consider what they say but make the effort to discover what we want and what we need to do. Our decision then comes from our own thoughtfulness and intelligence. We do not take what others say as our truth but discover what our truth is. By doing this we practice valuing ourselves and do not give our power away.

Practicing Respect Self also means that we set good boundaries and say no to others, even if it means we disappoint them. We gradually learn that saying no when necessary is a way to be kind to ourselves. We begin to see that saying no protects us from blindly following what others want or what they feel is best for us.

We also begin to discover what we are willing to compromise on and what we are not willing to compromise on. This has to do with developing a sense of honor and value. We become less willing to put ourselves in a position of being put down, controlled, or disrespected. In order for us to know what we are willing to compromise on we must find out what is vital to us; what is most important to us in *our* lives. What is vital to us is what nourishes us.

We become willing to be alone rather than be with people who diminish us. We learn how to manage our "aloneness" in a healthy way, enjoying our own company and seeking positive and wholesome activities and people to be with. We choose people to be friends with who are responsive, kind, and caring. But we are ok alone too, even if we are alone a lot we are ok, because we have a solid relationship with ourselves.

Our self-talk is kind, gentle, and encouraging. If it becomes negative and self-hating we notice this and stop and change to gentle self-talk.

We have discovered what we like and what we don't like. So instead of saying we'll go along with whatever our partner or friends suggest they want to do, we state our preferences. We can be decide that we really don't want to do something and are not willing to compromise at this time. We get clear and don't over explain ourselves. This may result in us staying home alone or going to the movies alone while our partner does what they want, but we are sure and confident enough within ourselves to make the best possible choice for us at that time.

Other aspects of Respect Self include not apologizing for being yourself; we *do* apologize for any hurtful or mindless behaviors. We stick up for ourselves in an assertive, not aggressive way even if someone may get mad. When we make a mistake we learn from it, let go, and move on. We accept ourselves while continuing to work at understanding ourselves.

We choose to live in ordered and clean surroundings, making an effort to make where we live as pleasant as possible no matter what our living arrangements are. Staying organized and tidy contributes to our sense of power and self-control while strengthening our self-discipline and self-regard.

In Respect Self we learn how to nurture ourselves and we gradually become our own best friend, thereby developing a relationship with ourselves that we can depend on and even be comforted with.

Real Life Stories

Carlie's Story: "Setting Boundaries"
Carlie offered to help some friends from her church load a truck because they were moving out of state. When she got to their house it was complete chaos. She sat around for over an hour waiting for them to get organized and spent twice as much time there as she had planned. She thought about all the valuable time she was wasting as she had put aside things she wanted to do for herself in order to help her friends.

About a month later another couple from church was moving and asked for help. Carlie told them she would be happy to help but this time announced that she would be available on such and such a day for 2 hours between 6:30 p.m. and 8:30 p.m. When she arrived, the first thing they did was offer a pizza dinner, even though she had eaten ahead of time thinking they would want to take advantage of her time there. She accepted the offer to sit with them. After eating they were ready to get things down from upstairs and start packing the truck. Carlie pitched in and at 8:30 p.m., even though there were big and difficult tasks left to do to load the truck, she said her good-byes. She felt good that she had helped and happy that she had the rest of the evening to do what she wanted to do. Her friends were grateful for her help and no one came away resentful.

June's Story: Recognizing her Over Explaining
One evening June wasn't feeling well and her husband said he was interested in seeing a new movie at the local theater. She really didn't want to see the movie that night, but remembered it was one of his favorite kinds of films. She felt badly for him but she knew it was better for her to stay at home and rest.

She said to her husband "Tonight is not a good night for me to go to the movie because I am not feeling well." Then, added, "but if you want to go alone that's ok." She realized as she said the last part, that it was not ok. She really wanted him to stay home with her and watch a DVD. She then began to explain herself more. He got irritated and expressed angrily that he had heard her. Then he explained that when she continued to go on and on with her explaining of why she didn't want to go he felt dumbed-down, and stupid. When June heard this she realized the effect of over explaining and stopped and then asked for what she really wanted – for them to spend the evening together relaxing at home and try for the movie later in the week.

Self-Reflection Exercise #1 for Respect Self

What we say to ourselves silently; self-talk like: "Boy, am I stupid!" has very powerful influence on what we believe about ourselves and how we feel. Part of learning how to honor and nurture ourselves is practicing encouraging and kind self-talk --- no matter what! Choose 3 of the Shaming-Busting Statements from the Appendix. Then write why you selected these three particular ones and describe how and when you will use them.

1.

2.

3.

Self-Reflection Exercise #2 Respect Self

Unresolved shamed and shame-anger spirals are centered around the "self". The self keeps looking at the self and becomes self-absorbed. We beat ourselves up and focus on how 'bad' we truly are (which is a lie). In order to lighten up and begin to create some emotional space from the unresolved shame we are wallowing in, it often works to shift the focus to something outside of ourselves. For example: A 20 minute walk (getting outside is healing); work in a garden; do some slow stretching exercises; do some yoga; do something simple for someone else (they don't even have to know!).

Below list some nurturing and safe ways you believe would "get you out of yourself." Practice some of them and make a note next to the ones that are most helpful.

1.

2.

3.

4.

Self-Reflection Exercise #3 Respect Self

Take a look at your close relationships, friendships, and acquaintances.

a) Reflect on how you can maintain healthy interactions in three important relationships, such as establishing boundaries, keeping the focus on yourself, and truly care for yourself.

Relationship One

_____

_____

_____

Relationship Two

_____

_____

_____

Relationship Three

_____

_____

_____

Self-Reflection Exercise #4 for Respect Self
Loving-kindness meditation for YOU.

Starting with 2 minutes for a sitting, then 5 minutes, then 15 minutes and on to 20 and 30 minutes do a loving-kindness meditation for yourself.

Instructions: Sit in a quiet place, no shoes, feet on floor, hands placed on top of legs, straight but relaxed and supported back, close your eyes and get in touch with your breathing. Follow your breath in, inhale, out, exhale. Do not force your breath, just feel its sensation.

Repeat the following phrase to yourself silently:

> May I be well.
> May I be happy.
> May I abide in peace.
> May I feel safe and secure.
> May I feel loved and cared for.

Self Reflection Exercise #5 for Respect Self

Draw or choose a picture of yourself in a magazine or internet picture that represents you as you see yourself in Respect Self: Focus on positive qualities, confidence, and assertiveness.

Awareness Exercises for Respect Self

Awareness of Body

a. Become aware of how you are standing when you are being assertive and saying what you mean and want to say.
b. Become aware of when you are keeping your head up, shoulders back and looking into people's eyes when you speak. Describe what body sensations occur. As you practice doing this do the body sensations change? How?
c. Describe your body sensation when you set a boundary with someone you always wanted to set a boundary with but never did.

Awareness of Thought and Speech

a. Using a log or note book record the number of times you notice positive self-talk for one week. Then, pick a few of your favorites from the Shame-Busting Statements in the Appendix and use them as your positive self-talk. Keep a record for the 2nd week. Has the number of times you use positive self-talk increased from week one?
b. Saying sorry is a habit that we keep on automatic. Keep a log about how often you say "sorry" each day for 7 days. By increasing your awareness of saying "sorry" were you able to decrease saying "sorry"? If not, keep a long for the next 7 days and see if it decreases. What have you replaced with saying "I'm sorry?"
c. Become aware when you are speaking clearly and with confidence.

Awareness of Feelings

a. Using the Feeling Faces in the Appendix start to become aware of 5 positive feelings you have every day. If you notice you have none or very few, pick one positive feeling and practice acting "as if" you are feeling it. Then try three more.
b. Make a conscious effort to discover what you really want when you need to make a choice during the day. Make one conscious choice a day for seven days without others' input. Then increase your effort by making three choices a day without others' input (best not to make it all food choices!). Write them down and next to each choice write how it felt to decide and choose for yourself. Use the Feeling Faces in the Appendix to help you identify your feelings.
c. Keep practicing using positive self-talk. Answer: Do I feel better about myself when I consciously use positive self-talk?

Practices for Respect Self

Start practicing these as often as possible. You start with one or several or all of them. Keep an inventory when practicing and check daily or weekly to see how it's going.

1. I say no assertively and when necessary, set healthy boundaries with others.

2. I am aware of my feelings and identified them most of the time.

3. I stick up for myself even though someone did not like it.

4. My self-talk is positive, encouraging and kind.

5. During a difficult time I choose to be kind and gentle to myself in a healthy way.

6. I accept myself while still seeking to understand myself and become more loving to myself.

7. When I make a mistake I work on self-acceptance and learn from it and let it go. I am honest with myself in a kind way.

8. I make self-caring and loving choices in my daily life.

9. I create as safe, clean and pleasant an environment as possible to live in.

10. I participate in activities that enhance my self-love and foster connection with others.

Present with Self

Here we are aware of how we feel at any one moment and use that as information to guide and regulate our behaviors. We choose to stay away from numbing behaviors and substances. We examine our part in difficult transactions with others, we maintain our honesty at all times, and we get our needs met by being assertive and forthright. The foundation is integrity and being congruent.

Present with Self

Present with Self means to stay with and observe uncomfortable feelings without reaching for the variety of substances and behaviors that get us numb or very distracted. Present with Self means that we start to develop an awareness of when and how we are avoiding what occurs inside of ourself. When we become aware of our avoidance tactics we are now entering Present with Self.

In Present with Self we stop deceiving ourself and move into honesty. This does not have to be done all at once, but we are entering Present with Self when we demonstrate the old behavior of a white lie, and then a half hour later fess up and tell the truth. Or, maybe we are thinking about manipulating someone into helping us with something, and we stop the manipulative thought and choose to ask for help. This opens us up to being vulnerable and asks you to be humble by realizing we need help and cannot do everything ourself. Asking requires us to extend ourself openly with others.

Present with Self requires breaking through denial by becoming aware and "waking up." For example, a person who drinks a lot says one day to a friend, "I think I might have a problem with alcohol. Things don't seem to go well when I drink." By saying that out loud to a friend this person has started to "wake up" to the possibility that they may have a drinking problem. This is moving toward being Present with Self.

Or, a friends says to you, "Why are you high again!? I don't like being around you when you are high." Somewhere inside you begin to think about your drinking and drugging. These personal reflections mean you are moving into Present with Self.

In this constellation, Present with Self means we pay attention and not dodge our feelings by drowning them in busyness, alcohol, drugs, shopping, or work. For example, reaching for a drink every time an emotion comes up suppresses the sensation of that emotion. How can we possibly get to understand what that emotion is telling you if it is suppressed with substance abuse or constant distractions? Reaching for a substance to control, suppress, regulate, manage, avoid, side-step, uncomfortable feelings, topics, and situations does not work. Discomfort just arises again (and again). Once again we will "reach for" or "do something" to avoid the discomfort. It's better to learn to ride-out the discomfort. In fact, it is emotionally strengthening to abide discomfort.

Being aware of our "avoidance tactics" is a lot easier to do when we are clean and sober. Abusing mind-altering substances confuses and hinders your efforts. Being "out of it," having a buzz on, getting high, being super busy, or being a workaholic does not lend itself to awareness of what is going on emotionally. We are not in the here and now when we are using. *Even if we use once in a while, during that time when we are using, we are not present with ourself.*

Awareness of our thoughts, feelings and body signals is clouded and blocked by using mind-altering substances. Drugs and alcohol create a fog of distortion making it difficult to find and use any self-honesty.

When we join the ranks of people that are clean and sober we will begin to notice how frequently we try to avoid discomfort. It is amazing how we can constantly use common things such as chocolate, shopping, fatty foods, talking a lot, reading all the time, being on the internet, or video games to keep away the discomfort of being in our own skin.

We are not talking here of periodic pleasant distractions, or taking a break from working hard all day by watching TV for part of an evening (every night all the time TV watching I would take a look at). We are talking about our intent. If our intent is to avoid consistently and constantly any unpleasantness then we need to look at what we are doing. We need to become aware that we are avoiding. Once we become aware of our avoidance tactics we are now entering Present with Self.

Present with Self means we stop "being on automatic" – doing things mindlessly and without awareness. We *check* to see if we are being manipulative, dishonest, deceitful or arrogant. We keep doing this check on ourself so that we are aware when we are getting "too full of ourself." We become straightforward and genuine in our interactions. This is called being forthright.

In Present with Self we do what it takes to not use on a daily (or hourly if necessary) basis. We are rigorously honest with ourself and others. Eventually we begin to value sobriety more than being high. We begin to feel more comfortable *not* using addictive substances. We start to embrace the truth about ourself. We also increase our tolerance for negative feelings such as shame, rage, anger, hurt, or sadness.

Real Life Stories

Clare's Story
I remember going on weight-watchers for several months. Initially I had a lot of strong uncomfortable feelings come up when I started changing my eating habits. I had to substitute a lot of fatty foods with non-fatty foods. I was amazed at the intensity of the emotional discomfort. Every emotion from discontent to sadness to anger came up full force. I felt also that I had lost a friend – "fatty-food-friend." Fatty foods are soothing. And, I had chosen to not to soothe my emotions with fatty foods so I could lose some weight. I remember clinging to the taste of jello chocolate non-fat pudding like it was a long-lost best friend! Eventually the emotional discomfort eased.

Ernesto's Story
I remember when I was unemployed for awhile but had a lot of projects to do. It was so much easier to just let myself read the news for a while on the internet instead of doing some serious job-search. I'd say to myself – well that article looks interesting – so I'd read it, then another one, and yet another one and soon an hour and a half had passed. Job searching is painful, it brings up uncomfortablenesses such as incompetence, inadequacy, frustration, confusion…need I say more. Reading the articles sucked me into "avoidance." I saw that I needed to use my time more wisely and tolerate the "uncomfortableness" of feeling powerless and inadequate as I stayed on the challenging task of job-search on-line. And, I needed to keep believing I was "enough."

Alice's Story
Sometimes the men in the drug and alcohol program I worked in would become very involved in projects for the unit or in helping others in the program – like doing a lot of tutoring. They often mentioned they realized they had stopped working on their own treatment plans when this happened. Too much involvement helped them avoid "themselves."

In AA and Alanon this can happen too when someone comes into the program and gets involved as a group representative or district rep and does lot of service or sponsors lots of people. They used these service activities to avoid focusing on the painful personal issues that may arise upon entering a 12 Step program.

Self-Reflection Exercise #1 for Present with Self

Describe five ways you made different choices in your actions when an uncomfortable feeling came up.

For example:

- Did you let yourself feel angry but not say anything until you calmly stated it later?
- Did you feel very disappointed and simply acknowledge this disappointment to someone instead of yelling, angrily complaining?
- Could you feel sad about something instead of the more intense feeling of devastation?
- Or, did you feel distressed about something and "sat" with the distress without reaching for a coffee, a cigarette, an ice cream/cake or other stronger substances?

1.

2.

3.

4.

5.

Self-Reflection Exercise #2 Present with Self

Describe your efforts in identifying your feelings.

a) Name three incidents when you have made an effort to discover what it is you were feeling.
b) Reflect on how noticing what you were feeling made a difference in your behavior.
c) Describe two times in the last month when you looked back on an incident and were able to recognize what feelings had come up.

Note: The Feeling Faces in the Appendix may help you recognize the feelings you are writing about.

Self-Reflection Exercise #3 Present with Self

Describe five different ways you can JUST BE and not fret, be busy, read, text, talk a lot, be on the internet, Facebook, twitter, or a cell phone. Reflect: a) What makes this difficult to do, i.e. what do you "crash into"? b) Practice getting in touch with your breath by sensing the inhale and the exhale (could be felt in your nostrils, throat, or tummy area).

1.

2.

3.

4.

5.

Self-Reflection Exercise #4 Present with Self

Draw or find a picture that shows you being Present with Self. Write five to ten characteristics around the picture to describe your Present with Self.

Awareness Exercises for Present with Self

Awareness of Body

a. Three times a day become aware of your general body sensations. Notice: Are you tired, hungry, need a stretch or need to move around or sit quietly. Take the time to attend to that by eating or drinking something nourishing, walking, or having a brief sit where you continue to pay attention to your body sensations.
b. Become aware when your body sensations indicate that your body is centered, nourished, and taken care of. Make a list of these body sensations and practice continually returning to them by re-adjusting your body.
c. Describe what feels satisfying to your body that does not entail any kind of substance such as alcohol, food, smoking or visual stimulation. Does warmth feel good, does a soft breeze feel good, does stretching feel good, does deep breathing feel good?
d. Practice getting in touch with your body sensation of breathing several times a day. This will help keep you in the present moment and self-aware.

Awareness of Thought and Speech

a. Using a log or note book record the number of healthy, straightforward, honest and level headed interactions you have with people in the course of a week. What types of phrases and words did you use? What could you do to make your communications even better?
b. Become aware of the thoughts you use to keep yourself honest (with yourself and others) Make a list of 10 thoughts that help you stay in integrity and help embrace the truth about yourself (without judgment).
c. Answer: How have I become more realistic and dropped the tendency to exaggerate?
d. Describe how you enjoyed your sobriety today.

Awareness of Feelings

a. Using the Feeling Faces in the appendix to pick out one feeling that you are *reasonably certain* you experienced today. Do this for two weeks. What patterns do you notice?
b. Sit for 2 to 5 minutes in the morning before breakfast, then 2 to 5 minutes in the evening. Notice what feelings arise. Do Not keep a log but become aware of the feeling. Use the Feeling Faces appendix to help identify them if you need to.
c. Notice what feelings come up when someone mentions a truth about you that you may or may not agree with.

Practices for Present with Self

Start practicing these as often as possible. You may start with one or several or all of them. Keep an inventory when practicing and check daily or weekly to see how it's going.

1. In a difficult or conflicted transaction I make a realistic assessment of my contribution to the situation.

2. When conversing with someone I stay on topic and stay interested.

3. I accept myself without reproach or excuses.

4. I get my needs met assertively, without whining, deceiving or manipulating others.

5. I appreciate nice things, but did not feel like I had to have them. I determine if I truly need to buy something or is it desire and want.

6. I relate to people as equals no matter their status in life.

7. I did not seek out drugs, alcohol or events that produce enormous excitement. I am content to participate in activities that do not produce a "rush."

8. I tolerate uncomfortable feelings without abusing a substance.

9. I am honest and straight forward in my personal and business transactions with others.

10. I do not have to have people know that I am right. I choose to be in the relationship more than having to be right.

Present with Others

Here *we* participate in our relationships, both personal and in the community. We contribute what we can and sometimes stretch ourselves to get involved in a positive way even when we would rather hide. We begin to believe that our contribution has value.

Present with Others

Present with Others shows up in our life on a daily basis by connecting, relating, giving in-put, and getting involved --- sometimes even when we don't really want to. Present with Others asks that we extend ourself in our personal relationships, work relationships, our living arrangements, and our neighborhood.

Being involved ranges from just making sure we are not neglectful of your responsibilities to being very active and engaged. Present with Others asks you to *stop* isolating or shying away from relating with others and respond to opportunities to enter into interactions with others.

Sometimes interactions with others gets very uncomfortable. We have all been in a situation where we really want to run out of the room and sometimes we do! The key to practicing Present with Others is staying and seeing the argument or uncomfortable encounter through to resolution if we can do so without harming (harm means emotionally and/or physically) ourself or others. It means more exposure for us, but this is the risk that moves us forward and builds our confidence.

One person identified a pattern of behavior as Hide from Others and because they became aware of that pattern started choosing to be more Present with Others. They said they did this by resolving to connect more with the people brought together in social situations and to add to this they chose to expand their professional experiences to be one of the best sales persons in their company. This took a conscious effort on their part to step into social and professional situations and be the first to begin the exchange in conversation.

Present with Others means we do not "duck" from our shame experiences. If we have enough guts to risk interactions, perhaps we will be fortunate enough to have a loving exchange with someone who provides a safe accepting space where we can practice being ourself. If we find ourself feeling awkward, inadequate, or incompetent it is extraordinarily healing to have a non-judgmental witness for us as we go through a shame-filled incident. We get a chance to show our humanness in front of others who accept and appreciate our humanness, and because *they* do, we start to accept ourselves.

Being Present with Others means that we stop hiding in a cocoon of any kind. Staying in a cocoon is easier in the electronic age with the internet, Facebook, streaming video, video games, iPhones, and even LinkedIn etc. All of that "electronic interaction" is deceiving. We believe we are connected (after all we have more than 500 electronic friends and connections!), but how often do we interact face-to-face? How often do they get to see us in person? It is in face-to-face interactions that Present with Others asks the most of us and in turn gives the most back to us.

A Real Life Story

Claire's Story
When Claire grew up her mother yelled and screamed at her if she didn't behave right in public. Her mother also yelled at her when she spilled something or lost something. Claire became very shy and isolated herself from others a lot. She had difficulty in relationships with boyfriends and felt very self-conscious when she made even little mistakes around them. Therefore she avoided being with people.

Eventually Claire married and one day in the kitchen there were 10 eggs in a carton on the wood island in the kitchen. Claire moved her hand and soon they crashed to the floor. She waited for her husband's response – the yelling and meanness that would come. But it didn't come. Instead he said, "They're just eggs. Accidents happen. We will get more."

Claire reported that she could feel the freedom and the healing as he said this. She felt lighter, and safer being Present with Others in other situations after this healing presence of her husband.

Self-Reflection Exercise #1 for Present with Others
Name five ways you will be able to grow personally (feel more freedom, feel safer, have more confidence) from more interaction and connection with others. Reflect: What are the possible *positive* outcomes of taking the risk to be a participant, relate to others openly on a regular basis, or accept support from others?

1.

2.

3.

4.

5.

Self-Reflection Exercise #2 Present with Others

Name five new *actions* you can take to reach out to others, get more involved at home, work, or in your community. With each new action write down one small step you can take to move forward with that new action, such as make a phone call, start saying hello to a neighbor, etc.

1. My new action:

My one small step to move forward:

2. My new action:

My one small step to move forward:

3. My new action:

My one small step to move forward:

4. My new action:

My one small step to move forward:

5. My new action:

My one small step to move forward:

Self-Reflection Exercise #3 Present with Others

Some of you may have started recovery from substance abuse. 12 Step programs encourage participants to "keep coming back" and to start, little by little to get involved with the group. Other self-help groups and volunteer groups encourage community involvement but sometimes it gets hard to keep going and not just stay home and veg (vegetate).

Write down five statements you can use on a regular basis as motivating self-talk to "keep coming back" with continued participation in your chosen group.

1.

2.

3.

4.

5.

Name five ways you will start to manage your time differently in order to honor your participation and commitments to your chosen groups.

1.

2.

3.

4.

5.

Self-Reflection Exercise #4 Present with Others
Draw a picture of yourself as you would like to interact with others as you continue to practice your Wise-Self in Present with Others.

Awareness Exercises for Present with Others

Awareness of Body

a. Notice your body sensations after reaching out to someone and interacting. Make a list of positive sensations and continue to note what your body sensation tells you during positive interactions.
b. Notice when you feel confident, especially with others. What is your posture? Your hand movements? Where do you let your eyes fall? How do you hold your head?
c. Practice getting in touch with your breath at least three times a day.

Awareness of Thought and Speech

a. Become aware of any ideas or thoughts you have about reaching out to others to connect or help solve a problem. What positive words can you say to yourself to encourage yourself to connect and ask for what you need or want?
b. Using a weekly or monthly log write down ways you have learned to talk with others in new social situations even though they were difficult. What were the outcomes.?
c. Using a weekly log list the number of times you have made a thoughtful effort to connect with others by participating with family, socializing with a friend, or going to community events, or going to AA /NA meetings instead of watching TV, being on the internet, or playing video games.

Awareness of Feelings

a. Using the Feeling Faces in the appendix to pick out one feeling that you are *reasonably certain* you experienced that day. Do this for two weeks. What patterns do you notice?
b. Using the Shame-Busting statements in the appendix pick one to say out loud 3 times a day into the mirror. Do this for four weeks, choosing a new statement for each week of that month. What feelings did you notice? What did you observe about your mood?
c. Notice what feelings come up when before going into a social event, what feelings occur during the social event, and what feelings occur after the event is over (when you may be alone again). Make a log of these feelings breaking it into the three categories above. What do you notice?

Practices for Present with Others

Start practicing these as often as possible. You may start with one or several or all of them. Keep an inventory when practicing and check daily or weekly to see how it's going.

1. I reach out for support and help rather than try to figure out solution by myself.

2. I choose to solve disagreements with people rather than hide and avoid them.

3. I participate in a least one activity involving other people.

4. I am socially active with thoughtful, kind and positive people.

5. I have regular contact with supportive, clean and sober reciprocal friends and acquaintances.

6. I work at maintaining my friendships, through phone, visits, and once in a while, an e-mail.

7. I am available to help others.

8. During an important interaction with someone I choose to stay in a conversation that is uncomfortable, choosing to leave when I finish what I need to say.

9. I have a good balance between alone-time and time with others.

10. I am a positive contributor to my neighborhood and community, even in a small way.

Appendices

The Vocabulary of Shame

One place to start with shame awareness is with the vocabulary of shame. This enables us to identify more clearly the uncomfortable thoughts and feelings that arise when shame arises. Shame can arise from an interaction or while alone just from the way you believe or see yourself. It is common to sense or feel a *combination* of the following:

- Flawed as a human being
- Unworthy
- Deficient and inadequate
- Lacking
- Not good enough
- No good and a bad person
- Wrong
- Discovered by others as "less than"
- Unsure and confused – all confidence in yourself is gone
- Disregarded, put down, put in your place
- Rejected and hurt
- Not heard or understood
- Humiliated, shamed, and dishonored
- A misfit with nothing to offer
- Pushed aside, excluded, left out, don't belong
- Foolish, stupid, dumb
- Cut off from your attempt to connect loss of dignity, self-respect, and pride

Exercise #1

1. Consider each word(s) in the list above carefully.
2. Be quiet and listen to what your feelings, thoughts and body tell you as you read the list.
3. Reflect on your interactions with others in your life and on how you see yourself.
4. Then, make a checkmark next to the descriptions that ring very true for you.

The Ranges of Shame

Exercise #2
As with most emotions shame can be very mild to very crippling; from weak to strong. Here is what one range of shame looks like with the less strong sense of shame on the left and the very strong sense of shame to the right:

Sample Range:

WEAKER   STRONGER
Shy - Embarrassed - Self-Conscious – Modest – Inadequate – Inferior – Disgraced – Dishonored –Disrespected – Humiliated -Mortified

The above is just one example of a shame-range. Everyone's is different because the meaning and strength of shame words are different for each one of us. The key is to find out what shame words *you* relate to and what you consider weaker or stronger.

Here is a list of more shame words to help you with Exercise:#2

- Vulnerable
- Emotionally Paralyzed
- Weak
- Defective
- Loser
- Helpless
- Low Self-esteem
- Hurt feelings
- Self-Doubt
- Hurt Pride

- Exposed
- Ignored
- Failure
- Stupid
- Flake
- Ugly
- Flawed
- Uncool
- Foolish
- Untrustworthy

Using any of the words that ring true for you make your own shame-range in the box below. You may do this exercise for several times for each specific situation that you want to reflect on.

Your shame-range here:

Weaker   Stronger

Shame Log

Day 1 Shame Log Intensity Low 0 1 2 3 4 5 6 7 8 9 High
Trigger

Shame Feeling that Came Up (see list)

Behavior

Day 2 Shame Log Intensity Low 0 1 2 3 4 5 6 7 8 9 High
Trigger

Shame Feeling that Came Up (see list)

Behavior

Day 3 Shame Log Intensity Low 0 1 2 3 4 5 6 7 8 9 High
Trigger

Shame Feeling that Came Up (see list)

Behavior

Day 4 Shame Log Intensity Low 0 1 2 3 4 5 6 7 8 9 High
Trigger

Shame Feeling that Came Up (see list)

Behavior

Day 5 Shame Log Intensity Low 0 1 2 3 4 5 6 7 8 9 High
Trigger

Shame Feeling that Came Up (see list)

Behavior

Alphabetical List of Shame Labels

Use these words on your shame log (if you want) where it says
"Shame Feeling that Came Up"

Affront
Alienated
Awkward
Bad
Bad character
Contemptible
Criticized
Defeated
Defective
Deficient
Demoralized
Dirty
Disappointed
Discouraged
Disrespected
Dissed
Embarrassed
Emotionally paralyzed
Envious
Exposed
Failure
Flake
Flawed
Foolish
Greedy
Guilty
Helpless
Humiliated
Hurt feelings
Hurt pride
Ignored
Imposter
Impotent
Indignant

Inferior
Inhibited
Insecure
Jealous
Lonely
Lose Face
Loser
Low self-esteem
Modest
Mortified
Poor
Prude
Private
Rejected
Self-conscious
Self-doubt
Sexless
Shame
Shy
Sick at heart
Sluttish
Stupid
Trivialized
Ugly
Uncool
Unlovable
Untrustworthy
Unworthy
Vulnerable
Weak
Wimp
Whore
Worthless

SHAME: SHOULD HAVE ALREADY MASTERED EVERYTHING

131

Shame-Busting Statements

1. Change flows like the seasons, and the universe can be trusted
2. I see life as a process, ever unfolding
3. I release my fear and resistance to change as appropriate
4. I release and forgive everyone who didn't support my changes
5. I release and heal all the changes that caused me pain
6. I forgive myself for making changes that didn't work
7. I forgive myself for not making changes that would have worked
8. I dissolve all past agreements that no longer serve me
9. I create new agreements that serve my new directions
10. I release all distress and worry
11. I release all negative thoughts and feelings.
12. I release all fear and anxiety
13. I release all stress and tension
14. I am loose and easygoing
15. I am in a state of ease and flow
16. I am relaxed and calm
17. I am serene and peaceful
18. I control my responses to stressful situations
19. I dissolve all negative responses to stressful situations
20. I respond to stressful situations in healthy and healing ways
21. I replace stress with calming thoughts
22. I replace stress with peaceful feelings
23. I replace stress with healthy habits
24. I am at peace whether or not I am in control
25. I am tranquil whether or not I know the future
26. I am calm whether or not things are going my way
27. I stand unshaken in my own serenity
28. I accept each situation without stressful reactions
29. I face every situation clear, free, and unafraid
30. I am now willing to move beyond my past
31. I release and forgive who I have been in the past
32. I release and forgive each person for who they have been in my past
33. I recognize who, what, and when to release and I do it
34. I dissolve all past issues in peace and grace
35. I understand the need to grieve and I do it as appropriate
36. I grieve for my past as appropriate
37. I grieve in healthy and healing ways
38. I grieve with people who are safe and supportive
39. I dissolve my denial in peace and harmony
40. I am safe and protected when I acknowledge all things in my life
41. I process my anger in healthy and healing ways
42. I dissolve my bargaining in peace and harmony
43. I release my depression quickly in grace
44. I move to acceptance in powerful new way

45. I am at peace with my past and how I have lived it
46. I accept the past is not my future
47. I release my past and live in my present
48. I live a powerful, forgiving life
49. I live a positive, loving life
50. I release and forgive everyone who created chaos in my life
51. I forgive myself for creating chaos
52. I know when to establish order and when to welcome chaos
53. I have faith in my future and myself
54. Everything I need comes to me
55. Everything I need to know is revealed to me
56. My security is in who I am, what I know, and what I believe
57. I trust my future and myself
58. I welcome my changes and my future
59. I move boldly forward with complete trust and faith
60. I face my unknown future wise, free, and unafraid
61. Communicating clearly and I are one
62. I dissolve all blocks to communicating clearly
63. It is natural for me to speak up for myself
64. I speak up for myself at the right times about the right things
65. I release and forgive everyone who put me down when I spoke up
66. I increase in assertiveness daily
67. I dissolve my passive characteristics as appropriate
68. I dissolve my aggressive characteristics as appropriate
69. I replace passive aggression with the power of clear communication
70. I say what I mean and I mean what I say
71. I increase in effective listening daily
72. I listen attentively, keeping an open, still mind
73. I create and participate in meaningful dialogs
74. I accept others completely when they express their feelings
75. Others accept me completely when I express my feelings
76. I am open and honest about my feelings and express them well
77. I recognize and acknowledge when I am feeling anger
78. I express my anger in healthy and healing ways for others and myself
79. As my communication increases in power, I increase in power
80. As I increase in power, my relationships increase in power
81. Getting what I want and I are one
82. I dissolve all confusion around what I want and need
83. I easily identify my wants and needs
84. I easily distinguish between what I want and what I need
85. I easily distinguish between my wants and the wants of others
86. I easily distinguish between my wants and what others want for me
87. I take myself and my wants and needs seriously
88. I put my needs first as appropriate
89. I am honest about what I want and need and I ask for it
90. I ask for what I want and need simply and clearly

91. I forgive everyone who didn't meet my needs
92. I take responsibility for my own needs
93. I assign others responsibility for their needs
94. I balance my needs with the needs of others in perfect ways
95. I tell others what I expect from them
96. I listen for what others expect from me
97. I make meaningful agreements and I keep them
98. I set appropriate limits and boundaries and I keep them
99. I have the courage to work through conflict to get what I want and need
100. I deal with whatever comes up in healthy and healing ways
101. I get what I want and need in all appropriate ways
102. I accept myself completely without qualifiers
103. I have a solid sense of self-identity
104. I see myself realistically and objectively
105. I find deep inner peace with myself as I am
106. I say positive things about myself to myself
107. I forgive myself for all I have done
108. I forgive every person in my life who has undermined my self-esteem
109. All of my false images of myself from the past are now dissolved
110. I love and accept all parts of myself
111. I love and accept all of my thoughts and feelings as part of myself
112. All false messages about me are now dissolved in total grace
113. I love and approve of myself aside from my accomplishments
114. I have positive self- esteem apart from others judgments and criticisms
115. I love and approve of myself without pleasing others
116. I accept myself completely as I am, though I recognize areas for improvement
117. I value and honor myself as I am, though I recognize areas for improvement
118. I am loving and accepting of who I am and who I am becoming
119. I stand firmly in my powerful positive self-esteem
120. I believe strongly in my powerful positive self-esteem
121. I feel total peace with my powerful positive self-esteem
122. I am secure and confident in myself
123. I discover, uncover, and recover aspects of my self-confidence daily
124. I maintain my self-confidence in all times and places
125. I balance my self-confidence with modesty in perfect ways
126. I dissolve all obstacles to having complete self-confidence
127. I heal all my issues around loss of self-confidence
128. I recognize and honor my true talents, abilities, and skills
129. I am confident of my capabilities, expertise, and know-how
130. I dissolve all false expectations of myself
131. I forgive myself for not living up to others expectations
132. I see each part of my life as a lesson in attitude and feeling
133. I forgive myself for any and all past mistakes
134. I dissolve all my fear around making mistakes
135. My self-confidence is in who I am, not what I do
136. I have faith in my future and myself

137. I stand firmly in my belief in myself
138. I believe in myself completely
139. I feel self-confident from the inside out
140. I am now filled with miracle consciousness
141. I move forward, feeling self-confident every step of the way
142. I open my heart to allow love in at all times
143. I open my heart to the magic of being alive
144. Life is a wondrous thing and I open my heart to celebrate it
145. I recognize the world as a safe and loving place
146. I reclaim my childlike ability to love without fear
147. I love others and myself unconditionally
148. I am loved and loving, and I rejoice in it
149. I hold the pattern of unconditional love and life flows easily
150. I dissolve all guards and shields I have around my heart
151. I dissolve all barriers to loving others and myself in peace and harmony
152. I release all pain and sadness from my heart in peace
153. I release all bitter experiences from my heart in peace
154. I release all fear and grief from my heart in peace
155. I connect with others and myself through my heart
156. I am safe on all levels as I go through life with my heart wide open
157. Only good can come to me when I open to give and receive love
158. I open to the power of people, places, and things to stir my heart
159. I surround myself with people with open, loving hearts
160. I have an infinite amount of love to share and I do so joyfully
161. I start my day with love, fill my day with love, and end my day with love
162. I accept myself completely as an imperfect person
163. I recognize criticism for what it is and I acknowledge it
164. I welcome valid criticism and I learn from it
165. I deflect false criticism and I respond appropriately
166. I forgive everyone who has criticized me
167. I forgive myself for criticizing others and myself
168. Being criticized and feeling attacked or inadequate are separate for me now
169. I dissolve all inappropriate responses to criticism
170. I dissolve all fear of being criticized
171. I dissolve all shame around being criticized
172. I dissolve all humiliation around being criticized
173. I respond to criticism in perfect ways for the situation and me
174. I feel loved and accepted while I handle criticism
175. I feel safe, secure, and supported while I handle criticism
176. I receive all criticism in peace and calmness
177. I am assertive and clear when I handle criticism
178. I remain calm, centered, and balanced while I handle criticism
179. My breathing stays deep and even while I handle criticism

Re-Printed with permission From Real Solution Anger Management Workbook
   Richard H. Pfeiffer, M.Div., LMFT
   You may purchase Richard's work from growthcentral.com

www.ingramcontent.com/pod-product-compliance
Lightning Source LLC
Chambersburg PA
CBHW080513110426
42742CB00017B/3097